Better Homes and Gardens

skinny slow cooker

More than **150** Calorie-Smart Recipes That Cook While You're Away

Meredith Corporation

Editor: Jan Miller

Project Editor: Lisa Kingsley, Waterbury Publications, Inc.

Contributing Editors: Tricia Bergman, Mary Williams, Waterbury Publications, Inc.

Contributing Writer: Laura Marzen, R.D.

Contributing Copy Editor: Terri Fredrickson

Contributing Proofreader: Gretchen Kauffman

Recipe Development: Carla Christian, Juli Hale

Recipe Testing: Better Homes and Gardens® Test Kitchen

Houghton Mifflin Harcourt

Publisher: Natalie Chapman

Editorial Director: Cindy Kitchel

Executive Editor: Anne Ficklen

Executive Editor: Linda Ingroia

Managing Editor: Marina Padakis Lowry

Director of Production: Tom Hyland

Design Director: Ken Carlson, Waterbury Publications, Inc.

Associate Design Director: Doug Samuelson, Waterbury Publications, Inc.

Production Assistant: Mindy Samuelson, Waterbury Publications, Inc.

Library of Congress Cataloging-in-Publication Data is available upon request.

ISBN: 978-1-118-56784-5 (pbk); ISBN 978-0-544-17846-5 (ebk)

Printed in the United States of America

DOW 10 9 8 7 6 5 4 3 2 1

4500450311

Our seal assures you that every recipe in *Better Homes and Gardens® Skinny Slow Cooker* has been tested in the Better Homes and Gardens® Test Kitchen. This means that each recipe is practical and reliable and meets our high standards of taste appeal. We guarantee your satisfaction with this book for as long as you own it.

Cover photo: Pasta with Eggplant Sauce, page 202

the nutrition breakdown

Each dish in this book is within a reasonable range of fat, calories, and fiber.

ENTRÉES

Calories: 425 or less
Fat: 15 grams or less
Protein: more than 10 grams
Fiber: 3 grams or more

SIDES AND SNACKS

Calories: 175 or less
Fat: 5 grams or less
Fiber: 1 gram or more

DESSERTS

Calories: 200 or less
Fat: 8 grams or less
Fiber: 1 gram or more

Look for icons indicating a recipe meets the following criteria:

● LOW CALORIE Main dishes with 300 calories or fewer per serving

● HIGH FIBER 5 or more grams per serving

● VEGETARIAN No ingredients contain meat or meat products

● GLUTEN FREE No ingredients contain gluten*

*__Gluten-free:__ These recipes can successfully be prepared with all gluten-free ingredients and may be suitable for people with celiac disease or other gluten sensitivities. Check the ingredient lists on all foods you use in these recipes to ensure they do not contain gluten.

get the skinny

Slow cookers make weeknight meals fuss-free because they do the work for you while you're busy living life. Alternatively, they provide an extra, hands-free cooking method while your stove top or oven is otherwise occupied, and their design means that foods emerge flavorful and tender. Still, when it comes to most slow-cooked comfort foods, making dishes that are delicious but also figure-friendly has been a challenge—until now.

In this collection of slimmed-down slow cooker recipes, you'll find more than 150 dishes to feed your family, your friends, or even a crowd. Each has been given the Better Homes and Gardens® Test Kitchen seal of approval, which means that each recipe has been tested for accuracy and tastes great. We employed smart cooking methods, ingredient swaps, and added lots of fresh produce. You will marvel that these recipes were made in a slow cooker.

From breakfast through the last sweet treat of the day—just wait until you taste the amazing 200-calorie-or-less desserts—this book will make sure you're well-nourished and well-fed. So get out your slow cooker and get ready to create healthful, balanced meals your whole family will love.

contents

slow cooker savvy

With low temperatures and an indirect heating source, slow cookers can safely cook meals for hours while you are off making use of your free time. Learn the basics of this cooking method and master the technique in no time.

back to basics

Fill the slow cooker liner at least half full and no more than two-thirds full.

Don't peek. Every time you open the lid, you release valuable moisture and add 30 minutes to the cooking time. There's no need to stir unless your recipe calls for it.

Beware of hot steam that gathers on the inside of the lid. To avoid burns, lift the lid gently and straight up without tilting until it's clear of the cooker.

Before washing your slow cooker, let the ceramic liner cool to room temperature to avoid cracking.

Slow cookers can fail to heat properly as they age.

Use this test to be sure your slow cooker is safe to use: Fill the slow cooker half to two-thirds full with water. Turn it on to the low-heat setting, then cover and heat for 8 hours. Check the water temperature with a food thermometer: It should register 185°F. If not, it's time to buy a new slow cooker.

veggie tales

Root vegetables, such as carrots, potatoes, and parsnips, are ideal for slow cooking. Add tender veggies—green beans, spinach, zucchini—at the end of cooking. Cook according to recipe directions or on the high-heat setting for 30 minutes or until veggies are tender.

Increase your vegetable intake by adding extra veggies to soups and stews—no one will notice the double dose.

meat matters

Always thaw frozen meat and poultry before cooking. Because of the slow rate of cooking, frozen meat will hover in the food-safety danger zone (40°F to 140°F) far too long.

To add flavor and color to your meat, brown it, drain off the excess fat, and then add the meat to the slow cooker.

skinny secrets

Here are the healthiest ways to trim down meals without sacrificing flavor. These 10 tips will turn you into a smarter cook.

1

Fresh and dried herbs can be swapped: 1 teaspoon dried herb equals 1 tablespoon fresh herb.

2

You can decrease or eliminate the amount of salt in a soup recipe by adding an acid such as lemon juice or vinegar toward the end of cooking. The acid makes up for lost flavor from cutting the salt.

3

Try using skinless chicken thighs. They stay moist and succulent during slow cooking, and they infuse the rest of the dish with rich-tasting flavor.

4 Trim excess fat from meat and poultry before cooking.

5

Save money (and sodium) by cooking your own dried beans. Cook extra and freeze surplus for later use.

6 Herbs—both fresh and dried—enhance the flavor of foods with no added calories. Add dried herbs early in the cooking process so their flavors have time to intensify and blend with other ingredients. Add fresh herbs at the end of cooking so they retain their bright flavor.

7 Buy an assortment of whole grains in bulk (available at your local health or whole foods store) and simplify their cooking by using your slow cooker.

8 To skim fat from hot cooking liquid before serving, dip a large metal spoon just below the surface of the liquid and allow the fat to stream into it. Discard the fat and continue skimming until most of the surface fat is removed.

To balance your nutrient intake, eat foods in a variety of colors throughout the the week.

9

A slow cooker can help you make meals more healthful by stretching small amounts of meat with flavorful sauces and a generous portion of vegetables.

10

breakfast

Sit down to a hearty hot cereal, breakfast pudding, or indulgent egg dish—healthful choices that give you energy all morning.

To ensure that the quiche cooks evenly, rotate it halfway through the cooking time to avoid overbrowning or uneven browning.

crustless spinach and mushroom quiche

PREP: 20 minutes   **SLOW COOK:** 5 hours (low) or 2 hours (high)   **COOL:** 15 minutes

Disposable slow cooker liner
Nonstick cooking spray
1 10-ounce package frozen chopped spinach, thawed and well drained
4 slices turkey bacon
1 tablespoon olive oil
2 cups coarsely chopped portobello mushrooms
½ cup chopped sweet red pepper (1 small)
1 cup shredded Gruyère or Swiss cheese (4 ounces)
8 eggs, lightly beaten, or 2 cups refrigerated or frozen egg product, thawed
2 cups reduced-fat milk
1 tablespoon snipped fresh chives or 1 teaspoon dried chives
¼ teaspoon salt
¼ teaspoon ground black pepper
½ cup reduced-fat biscuit mix

1. Line a 3½- or 4-quart slow cooker with disposable liner. Lightly coat liner with cooking spray. Press spinach with clean paper towels to remove as much liquid as possible; set aside.

2. In a medium skillet cook bacon until crisp; drain and crumble bacon. Set aside. Discard drippings. In the same skillet heat oil over medium heat. Add mushrooms and sweet pepper; cook and stir until tender. Stir in spinach and cheese.

3. In a medium bowl combine eggs, milk, chives, salt, and black pepper. Stir into spinach mixture in skillet. Gently fold in biscuit mix. Pour mixture into prepared slow cooker. Sprinkle with bacon.

4. Cover and cook on low-heat setting for 5 to 6 hours or on high-heat setting for 2 to 3 hours or until a knife inserted into center comes out clean. Turn off slow cooker. If possible, remove crockery liner from cooker. Cool for 15 to 30 minutes.

5. To serve, carefully lift disposable liner from cooker onto a cutting board. Remove quiche from disposable liner and slice to serve. **Makes 8 servings.**

PER SERVING: 243 cal., 15 g fat (6 g sat. fat), 237 mg chol., 455 mg sodium, 11 g carb., 1 g fiber, 17 g pro.

● LOW CALORIE

The favorite flavors of smoky sausage, spicy pepper Jack cheese, avocado, and salsa come together in this hearty frittata. Serve it with warmed whole wheat tortillas if you like.

southwestern frittata

PREP: 25 minutes   **SLOW COOK:** 2 hours (high)   **STAND:** 10 minutes

6   eggs
¾   cup chopped turkey smoked sausage
3   ounces shredded reduced-fat Monterey Jack cheese with jalapeño peppers (¾ cup)
¾   cup no-salt-added canned black beans, rinsed and drained
⅓   cup chopped red sweet pepper
¼   cup chopped red onion
1   fresh jalapeño, seeded and minced*
¼   teaspoon salt
    Nonstick cooking spray
1   medium avocado, peeled, seeded, and sliced
⅓   cup salsa

1. In a medium bowl lightly beat eggs. Add sausage, ½ cup of the cheese, the beans, sweet pepper, red onion, jalapeño, and salt. Lightly coat a 1½-quart souffle dish or casserole dish with nonstick spray. Transfer egg mixture into the prepared dish. Top with remaining ¼ cup cheese.

2. Place dish in the bottom of a 5- to 6-quart slow cooker. Cover and cook on high-heat setting for 2 to 2½ hours or until set and an instant-read thermometer inserted near the center registers 160°F. Let stand for 10 to 15 minutes.

3. Serve with avocado and salsa. **Makes 6 servings.**

*****Tip:** Because hot chile peppers contain volatile oils that can burn your skin and eyes, avoid direct contact with chiles as much as possible. When working with chile peppers, wear plastic or rubber gloves. If your bare hands do touch the chile peppers, wash your hands well with soap and water.

PER SERVING: 223 cal., 13 g fat (4 g sat. fat), 210 mg chol., 493 mg sodium, 9 g carb., 4 g fiber, 17 g pro.

Skip the line at the diner on a busy weekend morning and prepare this cheesy breakfast bake at home. This dish also makes great use of leftover ham.

ham, gouda, and potato bake

PREP: 20 minutes   **SLOW COOK:** 6 hours (low)

4   cups frozen diced hash brown potatoes

8   ounces reduced-sodium cooked ham, chopped

1   cup shredded Gouda cheese (4 ounces)

¾   cup chopped red sweet pepper (1 medium)

½   cup chopped onion (1 medium)

6   eggs, lightly beaten, or 1½ cups refrigerated or frozen egg product, thawed

1   10¾-ounce can condensed reduced-sodium cream of mushroom soup

½   cup fat-free milk

⅛   teaspoon ground black pepper

8   low-fat whole grain English muffins, split and toasted

1. In a 3½- or 4-quart slow cooker combine hash browns, ham, cheese, sweet pepper, and onion. Toss together until well mixed. In a medium bowl whisk together eggs, soup, milk, and black pepper. Pour over potato mixture in cooker.

2. Cover and cook on low-heat setting for 6 to 7 hours.

3. Serve ham mixture over English muffins. **Makes 8 servings.**

PER SERVING: 392 cal., 12 g fat (5 g sat. fat), 189 mg chol., 886 mg sodium, 53 g carb., 7 g fiber, 22 g pro.

cook smart Substitute your favorite flavor of cooked chicken sausage for the ham and try a different cheese, such as Fontina or cheddar, to turn this into a new dish. Your family will never know it's the same recipe!

For a milder-tasting dish, use condensed cheddar cheese soup instead of the nacho cheese soup.

loaded hash browns

PREP: 15 minutes   **SLOW COOK:** 8 hours (low) or 4 hours (high)

8 ounces uncooked bulk turkey sausage

8 ounces uncooked ground turkey breast

½ cup chopped onion (1 medium)
Disposable slow cooker liner

5 cups frozen diced hash brown potatoes

1 cup shredded reduced-fat Mexican-blend cheese (4 ounces)

1¼ cups chopped red sweet pepper (1 large)

1 4-ounce can (drained weight) sliced mushrooms, drained

1 medium fresh poblano pepper, seeded and chopped (see tip, page 14)

1 10¾-ounce can condensed fiesta nacho cheese soup

¼ cup water
Shredded reduced-fat Mexican-blend cheese (optional)
Thinly sliced fresh jalapeño pepper (see tip, page 14) (optional)
Salsa and/or light sour cream (optional)

1. In a large skillet cook sausage, ground turkey, and onion over medium heat until sausage is brown and onion is tender, using a wooden spoon to break up meat as it cooks. Drain off fat.

2. Line a 5- to 6-quart slow cooker with a disposable slow cooker liner. In prepared slow cooker combine sausage mixture, hash browns, the 1 cup cheese, the sweet pepper, mushrooms, and poblano pepper. In a medium bowl combine soup and the water. Pour over hash brown mixture in cooker; stir to combine.

3. Cover and cook on low-heat setting for 8 to 9 hours or on high-heat setting for 4 to 4½ hours.

4. Stir before serving. If desired, top with additional cheese and sliced jalapeño peppers. If desired, serve with salsa and/or sour cream. **Makes 8 servings.**

PER SERVING: 371 cal., 12 g fat (5 g sat. fat), 62 mg chol., 833 mg sodium, 41 g carb., 4 g fiber, 26 g pro.

This update on a classic hash has the feel of a stick-to-your-ribs dish but with fewer calories.

red flannel hash

PREP: 20 minutes   **SLOW COOK:** 6 hours (low) or 3 hours (high)

4½ cups round red potatoes, peeled and chopped (1½ pounds)

1½ pounds beets, peeled and chopped

12 ounces cooked corned beef from deli (about ¾-inch-thick chunk), chopped

1 cup chopped onion (1 large)

¼ cup reduced-sodium beef broth or reduced-sodium chicken broth

2 tablespoons spicy brown mustard

2 tablespoons butter, melted

1 tablespoon honey

1 tablespoon cider vinegar

¼ teaspoon salt

½ teaspoon bottled hot pepper sauce

¼ teaspoon ground black pepper

1. In a 3½- or 4-quart slow cooker combine potatoes, beets, corned beef, onion, broth, mustard, butter, honey, vinegar, salt, hot pepper sauce, and pepper.

2. Cover and cook on low-heat setting for 6 to 7 hours or on high-heat setting for 3 to 3½ hours. Stir before serving. **Makes 6 servings.**

PER SERVING: 257 cal., 5 g fat (3 g sat. fat), 35 mg chol., 908 mg sodium, 39 g carb., 6 g fiber, 15 g pro.

cook smart If you're not accustomed to the pronounced flavor of corned beef, try using half deli roast beef and half deli corned beef for a milder taste.

If you like your cereal slightly less sweet, try using plain yogurt instead of vanilla.

good-morning oatmeal

PREP: 15 minutes **SLOW COOK:** 6 hours (low)

3	cups water
1¾	cups apple juice
1½	cups steel-cut oats
1	medium pear, cored and chopped
1	7-ounce package mixed dried fruit bits
⅓	cup packed brown sugar
½	teaspoon salt
½	teaspoon ground cinnamon
2	6-ounce cartons vanilla Greek fat-free yogurt
1	cup low-fat granola (optional)

1. In a 3½- or 4-quart slow cooker combine the water, apple juice, oats, pear, fruit bits, brown sugar, salt, and cinnamon.

2. Cover and cook on low-heat setting for 6 to 7 hours.

3. Serve topped with yogurt and, if desired, granola. **Makes 6 servings.**

PER SERVING: 393 cal., 3 g fat (0 g sat. fat), 3 mg chol., 259 mg sodium, 82 g carb., 9 g fiber, 11 g pro.

cook smart Steel-cut oats are a must for this hearty breakfast cereal. They will stand up to the long cook time better than rolled oats, and, as a bonus, provide twice as much fiber compared with the same measure of rolled oats.

Be sure to rinse the quinoa before using it to remove a natural coating that can be slightly bitter—and use a very fine-mesh strainer or the grains will fall right through the holes and down the drain!

mixed-berry breakfast quinoa

PREP: 15 minutes   **SLOW COOK:** 4 hours (low) or 2½ hours (high)

2	**very ripe bananas, peeled**
4	**cups water**
2	**cups quinoa, rinsed and drained**
1	**12-ounce package frozen mixed berries**
2	**tablespoons packed brown sugar**
2	**teaspoons vanilla**
½	**teaspoon ground cinnamon**
¼	**teaspoon salt**
½	**cup chopped walnuts, toasted***

1. Place bananas in a 3½- or 4-quart slow cooker. Using a fork, mash bananas. Stir in the water, quinoa, mixed berries, brown sugar, vanilla, cinnamon, and salt.

2. Cover and cook on low-heat setting for 4 to 5 hours or on high-heat setting for 2½ hours. Sprinkle individual servings with walnuts. **Makes 8 servings.**

*Tip: To toast whole nuts or large pieces, spread them in a shallow pan. Bake them in a 350°F oven for 5 to 10 minutes, shaking the pan once or twice. (For hazelnuts, let them cool slightly, then place the warm nuts on a clean kitchen towel; rub with the towel to remove the loose skins.) Toast coconut in the same way, but watch it closely to avoid burning it. Toast finely chopped or ground nuts, pine nuts, or sesame seeds in a dry skillet over medium heat. Stir often so they don't burn.

PER SERVING: 244 cal., 5 g fat (1 g sat. fat), 0 mg chol., 76 mg sodium, 43 g carb., 6 g fiber, 7 g pro.

cook smart Quinoa may look humble, but it boasts being one of the most nutrient-dense of all grains. Not only is it higher in protein than many other grains, it is also lower in carbohydrate than many other grains, making it an excellent choice for weight management. With its mild, nutty flavor, it will work well in many of your favorite grain-based recipes.

This is multigrain cereal at its best. A blend of steel-cut oats, cracked wheat, brown rice, barley, millet, and cornmeal simmers into one creamy, hearty hot dish sweetened with dried fruit.

six-grain slow cooker porridge

PREP: 15 minutes   **SLOW COOK:** 6 hours (low)

5   **cups water**
1   **cup mixed dried fruit, coarsely snipped, and/or dried cranberries, dried tart cherries, and/or raisins (about 7 ounces)**
¼   **cup chopped crystallized ginger**
3   **tablespoons steel-cut oats**
3   **tablespoons cracked wheat**
3   **tablespoons regular brown rice**
2   **tablespoons regular barley**
2   **tablespoons millet or regular brown rice**
2   **tablespoons yellow cornmeal**
1   **teaspoon ground cinnamon**
1   **teaspoon vanilla**
¼   **teaspoon salt**
¾   **cup chopped pecans, toasted (see tip, page 23)**
    Fat-free milk
    Turbinado sugar, maple syrup, and/or shredded coconut (optional)

1. In a 3½- or 4-quart slow cooker combine the water, dried fruit, ginger, oats, cracked wheat, uncooked brown rice, barley, millet, cornmeal, cinnamon, vanilla, and salt.

2. Cover and cook on low-heat setting for 6 to 7 hours. Stir before serving. If too thick, stir in a bit of boiling water.

3. Top each serving with 2 tablespoons pecans, some milk, and, if desired, turbinado sugar, maple syrup, and/or shredded coconut. **Makes 6 servings.**

PER SERVING: 325 cal., 11 g fat (1 g sat. fat), 2 mg chol., 175 mg sodium, 51 g carb., 6 g fiber, 9 g pro.

Hearty steel-cut oats will fill you up and keep you going throughout the morning. Look for them near the old-fashioned oats in your grocery store.

cranberry-maple oatmeal with pears

PREP: 15 minutes   **SLOW COOK:** 6 hours (low)

	Nonstick cooking spray
4¾	cups water
1½	cups steel-cut oats
⅓	cup pure maple syrup
⅓	cup golden raisins
⅓	cup dried cranberries
⅓	cup chopped dried pears
1	teaspoon ground cinnamon or five-spice powder
1	teaspoon vanilla
½	teaspoon salt
	Milk (optional)

1. Lightly coat the inside of a 3½- or 4-quart slow cooker with cooking spray. In prepared slow cooker combine the water, oats, syrup, raisins, cranberries, pears, cinnamon, vanilla, and salt.

2. Cover and cook on low-heat setting for 6 to 7 hours. If desired, serve with milk. **Makes 8 servings.**

PER SERVING: 198 cal., 2 g fat (0 g sat. fat), 0 mg chol., 152 mg sodium, 44 g carb., 4 g fiber, 5 g pro.

cook smart Don't be tempted to use a low-calorie maple-flavored syrup in place of the pure maple syrup to save calories. The low-calorie syrup may contain artificial sweeteners that won't hold up to the long cook time, causing them to lose sweetness. The result can be a bitter, off flavor that you don't need to start your day!

● HIGH FIBER ● VEGETARIAN

Homemade granola toasts just as well in the slow cooker as it does in the oven—and you can leave the house as it cooks. Spreading it out on a sheet pan allows it to get pleasingly crunchy as it cools.

slow-toasted granola

PREP: 20 minutes **SLOW COOK:** 2½ hours (high)

½	cup honey
½	cup applesauce
¼	cup canola oil
¼	cup peanut butter
1	teaspoon ground cinnamon
	Nonstick cooking spray
5	cups regular rolled oats
½	cup sunflower kernels
¼	cup flaked coconut
2	tablespoons ground flaxseeds or wheat germ
½	cup golden raisins
¼	cup chopped pitted dates

1. In a small bowl whisk together honey, applesauce, canola oil, peanut butter, and cinnamon.

2. Lightly coat a 3½- or 4-quart slow cooker with cooking spray. In the slow cooker combine oats, sunflower kernels, coconut, and flaxseeds. Add honey mixture and stir to coat.

3. Place the lid offset on the slow cooker to vent it. Cook on high-heat setting 2½ hours or until toasted, stirring every 30 minutes.

4. Spread granola on a sheet pan to cool. Stir in raisins and dates. Store in an airtight container for up to 5 days or freeze up to 2 months. **Makes 16 servings.**

PER SERVING: 337 cal., 12 g fat (2 g sat. fat), 0 mg chol., 39 mg sodium, 51 g carb., 7 g fiber, 10 g pro.

cook smart The nutritional benefits of flaxseeds are more available to your body when you use ground flaxseeds as opposed to whole seeds. You can find ground flaxseeds in most supermarkets or health food markets. Or grind your own seeds using a clean coffee or spice grinder.

Look for whole grain waffles with 5 or more grams of fiber per serving for a filling and heart-healthy breakfast.

gingered fruit-topped waffles

PREP: 20 minutes   **SLOW COOK:** 6 hours (low) or 3 hours (high)

3	medium pears, peeled (if desired), cored, and cubed
1	20-ounce can pineapple chunks (juice pack), undrained
2	cups frozen unsweetened pitted dark sweet cherries
¾	cup dried apricots, quartered
2	tablespoons frozen orange juice concentrate, thawed
2	tablespoons packed brown sugar
1	tablespoon quick-cooking tapioca
1	tablespoon grated fresh ginger or 1 teaspoon ground ginger
16	frozen low-fat, whole wheat waffles, toasted
¼	cup chopped pecans, toasted (see tip, page 23) (optional)

1. In a 3½- or 4-quart slow cooker combine pears, pineapple, cherries, apricots, orange juice concentrate, brown sugar, tapioca, and ginger.

2. Cover and cook on low-heat setting for 6 to 8 hours or on high-heat setting for 3 to 4 hours. Spoon hot fruit mixture over hot toasted waffles. If desired, sprinkle with pecans. **Makes 8 servings.**

PER SERVING: 299 cal., 2 g fat (0 g sat. fat), 0 mg chol., 395 mg sodium, 69 g carb., 7 g fiber, 6 g pro.

● LOW CALORIE ● VEGETARIAN

This gooey bread pudding only looks decadent. At just 231 calories and 5 grams of fat per serving, you can enjoy it with abandon—and often!

french toast bread pudding

PREP: 15 minutes **CHILL:** 4 hours **SLOW COOK:** 7 hours (low) **COOL:** 30 minutes

	Disposable slow cooker liner
12	ounces challah or sweet bread (such as Portuguese or Hawaiian sweet bread), cut into 1-inch cubes (about 9 cups)
4	cups fat-free milk
½	cup sugar
3	eggs, lightly beaten, or ¾ cup refrigerated or frozen egg product, thawed
1	teaspoon vanilla
¼	teaspoon salt
	Sugar-free caramel ice cream topping, warmed

1. Line a 3½- or 4-quart slow cooker with a disposable slow cooker liner. Place bread cubes in prepared slow cooker.

2. In a large bowl whisk together milk, sugar, eggs, vanilla, and salt. Pour over bread cubes in cooker. Press bread down lightly with back of a large spoon to moisten bread completely. Cover and chill in the refrigerator for 4 to 24 hours.

3. Cover and cook on low-heat setting for 7 to 8 hours or until a knife inserted in the center comes out clean. Turn off cooker. If possible, remove crockery liner from cooker. Cool for 30 minutes.

4. To serve, carefully lift disposable liner from cooker. Using a plate, transfer French toast to a cutting board; slice French toast. (Or, if desired, spoon it into serving dishes.) Top with ice cream topping. **Makes 12 servings.**

PER SERVING: 231 cal., 5 g fat (2 g sat. fat), 33 mg chol., 287 mg sodium, 39 g carb., 1 g fiber, 7 g pro.

appetizers, snacks & drinks

These dips, wings, snack mixes, and steaming drinks practically cook themselves, which makes hosting your next special event a breeze.

These delicious wings with a slightly kicky peanut sauce turn any gathering into a party.

thai chicken wings with peanut sauce

PREP: 25 minutes   **SLOW COOK:** 5 hours (low) or 2½ hours (high)

24	chicken drumettes (about 2¼ pounds total)
¼	cup water
1	tablespoon lime juice
¼	teaspoon ground ginger
1	recipe Peanut Sauce

1. In a 3½- or 4-quart slow cooker combine chicken, the water, lime juice, and ginger.

2. Cover and cook on low-heat setting for 5 to 6 hours or on high-heat setting for 2½ to 3 hours.

3. Drain chicken, discarding cooking liquid. Toss chicken with half of the Peanut Sauce. If desired, return chicken to slow cooker. Serve immediately or keep warm, covered, on warm or low-heat setting for up to 1 hour. Serve with remaining Peanut Sauce (whisk sauce if it looks separated). **Makes 12 servings.**

Peanut Sauce: In a small saucepan whisk together ½ cup creamy peanut butter; ½ cup water; 2 tablespoons reduced-sodium soy sauce; 2 cloves garlic, minced; ½ teaspoon ground ginger; and ¼ teaspoon crushed red pepper. Heat over medium-low heat until mixture is smooth, whisking constantly. Makes about 1 cup.

PER SERVING: 101 cal., 6 g fat (1 g sat. fat), 15 mg chol., 159 mg sodium, 3 g carb., 1 g fiber, 9 g pro.

cook smart A chicken drumette is the meatiest of the three sections of the chicken wing. If you can't find them already cut for you in the freezer or poultry section of the supermarket, you can cut your own using fresh chicken wings. Cut the wing into three sections where the bones meet. Discard the tips and save the middle section for another use.

The sweet and spicy molasses-lime sauce will keep guests from knowing that there are good-for-you oats in these party meatballs.

molasses-lime meatballs

PREP: 30 minutes   **SLOW COOK:** 4 hours (low) or 2 hours (high)

Nonstick cooking spray
1½   pounds extra-lean ground beef
8   ounces uncooked hot Italian turkey sausage links, casings removed
1   cup quick-cooking rolled oats
1   cup refrigerated or frozen egg product, thawed, or 4 eggs, lightly beaten
1   cup finely chopped green onions (8)
4   teaspoons Worcestershire sauce
1   teaspoon crushed red pepper
6   tablespoons molasses
¼   cup reduced-sodium soy sauce
2   tablespoons lime juice

1. Coat a 3½- or 4-quart slow cooker with cooking spray; set aside. In a large bowl combine ground beef, sausage, oats, egg product, green onions, Worcestershire sauce, and crushed red pepper. Shape mixture into 72 approximately 2-inch meatballs.

2. Coat a very large nonstick skillet with cooking spray. Cook meatballs, one-fourth at at time, over medium heat until brown, turning once. Transfer to prepared cooker.

3. Cover and cook on low-heat setting for 4 to 5 hours or on high-heat setting for 2 to 2½ hours.

4. In a small bowl whisk together molasses, soy sauce, and lime juice. Pour over meatballs. Toss gently to coat. Serve immediately or keep warm, covered, on warm or low-heat setting for up to 1 hour. **Makes 16 servings.**

PER SERVING: 140 cal., 4 g fat (2 g sat. fat), 34 mg chol., 350 mg sodium, 12 g carb., 1 g fiber, 14 g pro.

cook smart Meatballs are often made using bread crumbs. Opting for oats, like this recipe uses, adds cholesterol-lowering soluble fiber and a host of other beneficial nutrients that you wouldn't get from bread crumbs.

This hearty dip is fashioned after picadillo (pee-kah-DEE-yoh), a Latin mélange of meat, garlic, sweet spices, almonds, and raisins that is often served with beans and rice or as a stuffing.

picadillo dip

PREP: 20 minutes   **SLOW COOK:** 6 hours (low) or 3 hours (high)

1   **pound ground beef**
1   **16-ounce jar salsa**
½   **cup chopped onion (1 medium)**
½   **cup raisins**
¼   **cup sliced pimiento-stuffed olives**
2   **tablespoons red wine vinegar**
3   **cloves garlic, minced**
½   **teaspoon ground cinnamon**
½   **teaspoon ground cumin**
¼   **cup slivered almonds, toasted (see tip, page 23)**
     Slivered almonds, toasted (see tip, page 23) (optional)
     Toasted pita wedges or bagel chips

1. In a large skillet cook ground beef until brown, using a wooden spoon to break up meat as it cooks. Drain off fat. In a 3½- or 4-quart slow cooker combine ground beef, salsa, onion, raisins, olives, vinegar, garlic, cinnamon, and cumin.

2. Cover and cook on low-heat setting for 6 to 8 hours or on high-heat setting for 3 to 4 hours.

3. Stir in the ¼ cup almonds. If desired, sprinkle with additional almonds. Serve with toasted pita wedges. Serve immediately or keep warm, covered, on warm or low-heat setting for up to 2 hours. **Makes 16 servings.**

PER SERVING: 94 cal., 5 g fat (2 g sat. fat), 18 mg chol., 217 mg sodium, 7 g carb., 1 g fiber, 7 g pro.

The stronger flavor of the Asiago cheese means you can use lower-fat mayo and sour cream and still have a rich-tasting dip with a smooth and creamy texture.

asiago cheese dip

PREP: 25 minutes   **SLOW COOK:** 3 hours (low) or 1½ hours (high)

1 cup chicken broth or water

4 ounces dried tomatoes (not oil-packed)

2 16-ounce cartons light sour cream

1 cup finely shredded Asiago cheese (4 ounces)

1¼ cups light mayonnaise or salad dressing

1 cup sliced fresh mushrooms or 1 ounce dehydrated dried mushrooms, such as porcini, shiitake, chanterelle, and/or oyster, coarsely chopped*

1 cup thinly sliced green onions (8)

½ of an 8-ounce package light cream cheese (Neufchâtel), cut up

Thinly sliced green onions

Whole grain baguette-style French bread slices, toasted**

1. In a small saucepan bring broth to boiling. Remove from heat. Add tomatoes; cover and let stand for 5 minutes. Drain, discarding liquid. Chop tomatoes (you should have about 1¼ cups).

2. Meanwhile, in a 3½- or 4-quart slow cooker combine sour cream, Asiago cheese, mayonnaise, mushrooms, the 1 cup green onions, and the cream cheese. Stir in tomatoes.

3. Cover and cook on low-heat setting for 3 to 4 hours or on high-heat setting for 1½ to 2 hours.

4. Stir well before serving. Sprinkle dip with additional green onions and serve with toasted bread slices. Serve immediately or keep warm, covered, on warm or low-heat setting for up to 2 hours. **Makes 52 servings.**

*Tip: To rehydrate dried mushrooms, place the dried mushrooms in a small bowl. Add enough boiling water to cover; let stand for 30 minutes. Drain mushrooms, squeezing out any excess liquid. Coarsely chop mushrooms.

**Tip: To toast bread slices, preheat broiler. Place bread slices on a large baking sheet. Broil 3 to 4 inches from heat for 2 to 3 minutes or until toasted, turning once.

PER SERVING: 65 cal., 5 g fat (2 g sat. fat), 12 mg chol., 140 mg sodium, 3 g carb., 0 g fiber, 2 g pro.

cook smart If you choose to use the dried mushroom option, save the rehydrating liquid after draining the mushrooms. Use it in place of some of the broth in sauces or soups to add depth to the flavor without added sodium.

This lightened-up, slow cooker version of a wildly popular party dip gets spiciness from cayenne and tang from fresh lemon juice.

spinach-parmesan dip

PREP: 10 minutes **SLOW COOK:** 2½ hours (low) or 1½ hours (high)

Nonstick cooking spray
2 10-ounce packages frozen chopped spinach, thawed
1 14-ounce can quartered artichoke hearts, drained and coarsely chopped
1 cup chopped onion (1 large)
1 tablespoon Dijon mustard
4 cloves garlic, minced
½ teaspoon dried oregano, crushed
¼ teaspoon cayenne pepper
½ cup light mayonnaise or salad dressing
½ cup fat-free sour cream
¼ cup shredded Parmesan cheese (1 ounce)
¼ cup shredded Italian cheese blend (1 ounce)
1 tablespoon lemon juice

1. Coat a 3½- or 4-quart slow cooker with cooking spray; set aside. Squeeze spinach dry, reserving ⅓ cup spinach liquid. In prepared cooker combine spinach, the ⅓ cup liquid, artichokes, onion, mustard, garlic, oregano, and cayenne pepper.

2. Cover and cook on low-heat setting for 2½ to 3 hours or on high-heat setting for 1½ hours. Turn off cooker; stir in mayonnaise, sour cream, Parmesan cheese, Italian cheese blend, and lemon juice. **Makes 16 servings.**

PER SERVING: 66 cal., 4 g fat (1 g sat. fat), 5 mg chol., 229 mg sodium, 6 g carb., 2 g fiber, 3 g pro.

cook smart Using canned artichokes takes the intimidation away from using fresh artichokes, making this dip a cinch to prepare. Artichokes are high in fiber at 7 grams per ½ cup cooked, making this dip not only delicious but nutritious, too.

A warm bath in red wine, butter, brown sugar, garlic, and dill gives these mushrooms outstanding flavor. Their natural meatiness makes them feel heartier than a scant 50 calories per serving would suggest.

marinated mushrooms

PREP: 20 minutes   **SLOW COOK:** 8 hours (low) or 4 hours (high)

2   pounds assorted mushrooms such as stemmed shiitakes, cremini, and/or button mushrooms

1   8- to 9-ounce package frozen artichoke hearts

1   14½-ounce can lower-sodium beef broth

1   cup red Zinfandel or other dry red wine

2   tablespoons butter, cut up

1   tablespoon packed brown sugar

1   tablespoon Worcestershire sauce

2   cloves garlic, minced

1   teaspoon dried dill weed

1. In a 5- to 6-quart slow cooker combine mushrooms and artichokes. Add broth, wine, butter, brown sugar, Worcestershire sauce, garlic, and dill weed.

2. Cover and cook on low-heat setting for 8 to 10 hours or on high-heat setting for 4 to 5 hours. Serve warm or chill and serve cold. **Makes 16 servings.**

PER SERVING: 50 cal., 2 g fat (1 g sat. fat), 4 mg chol., 76 mg sodium, 5 g carb., 1 g fiber, 2 g pro.

cook smart Mushrooms have a lot to boast about: Not only are they super satisfying with their earthy flavor and meaty texture, they can boast being the only fresh fruit or vegetable that contains vitamin D. It's available in only a few foods and is a fat-soluble vitamin necessary for the promotion of calcium absorption and bone growth.

Traditional aïoli is a garlicky mayonnaise-based sauce served with grilled, roasted, or steamed vegetables, meat, or fish. This version is based on sour cream infused with garlic, horseradish, onion, and dill.

party potatoes with creamy aïoli

PREP: 25 minutes **SLOW COOK:** 6 hours (low) or 3 hours (high)

Nonstick cooking spray
2 pounds tiny new potatoes
1 red onion, cut into thin wedges
½ cup reduced-sodium chicken broth
2 cloves garlic, minced
½ teaspoon smoked paprika or regular paprika
¼ cup finely chopped green onions (2)
¼ teaspoon salt
¼ teaspoon ground black pepper
1 8-ounce carton light sour cream
1 tablespoon prepared horseradish
1 tablespoon finely chopped onion
1 tablespoon snipped fresh dill or 1 teaspoon dried dill weed
2 cloves garlic, minced
½ teaspoon salt

1. Coat a 3½- or 4-quart slow cooker with cooking spray. Halve or quarter any large potatoes. Place potatoes and onion wedges in prepared cooker. In a small bowl stir together broth, 2 cloves garlic, and paprika. Pour over potatoes and onion in cooker.

2. Cover and cook on low-heat setting for 6 to 7 hours or on high-heat setting for 3 to 3½ hours. Place potato mixture in a serving bowl; toss with green onions, the ¼ teaspoon salt, and pepper.

3. Meanwhile, for aïoli, in a small bowl whisk together sour cream, horseradish, chopped onion, dill, 2 cloves garlic, and ½ teaspoon salt. Cover with plastic wrap; chill until serving time.

4. Serve potatoes warm or at room temperature with the aïoli. **Makes 8 servings.**

PER SERVING: 132 cal., 3 g fat (2 g sat. fat), 8 mg chol., 284 mg sodium, 24 g carb., 3 g fiber, 4 g pro.

The feisty flavor from lemon peel and herbs guarantees this party mix will be a hit. The well-balanced ratio of carbohydrate to protein and fat also makes it a good pack-and-go snack.

lemon-zested snacker mix

PREP: 15 minutes   **SLOW COOK:** 2½ hours (low) or 80 minutes (high)

Nonstick cooking spray
5 cups bite-size multigrain or wheat square cereal
2 cups plain pita chips, broken into bite-size pieces
⅔ cup chopped walnuts
¼ cup pumpkin seeds (pepitas)
1 1-ounce packet dry ranch salad dressing mix
2 tablespoons dried dill weed
1 teaspoon dried rosemary, crushed
2 tablespoons olive oil
1 tablespoon finely shredded lemon peel

1. Lightly coat a 5- to 6-quart slow cooker with cooking spray. In prepared slow cooker combine cereal, pita chips, walnuts, pumpkin seeds, salad dressing mix, dill weed, and rosemary. Drizzle mixture with oil, tossing gently to blend.

2. Cover and cook on low-heat setting for 2½ hours, stirring every 40 minutes, or on high-heat setting for 80 minutes, stirring every 20 minutes.

3. Sprinkle lemon peel over mixture, tossing gently to blend. Spread mixture in an even layer on a 13×9×2-inch baking sheet; cool completely. Store in an airtight container for up to 2 weeks. **Makes 24 servings.**

PER SERVING: 107 cal., 5 g fat (1 g sat. fat), 0 mg chol., 209 mg sodium, 15 g carb., 2 g fiber, 2 g pro.

If you happen to have some of these lively nuts left over, sprinkle them on salads or serve with a ripe fresh pear and some cheese for dessert.

five-spice pecans

PREP: 10 minutes   **SLOW COOK:** 2 hours (low)

1	pound pecan halves, toasted (4 cups) (see tip, page 23)
¼	cup butter or margarine, melted
2	tablespoons soy sauce
1	teaspoon five-spice powder
½	teaspoon garlic powder
½	teaspoon ground ginger
¼	teaspoon cayenne pepper

1. Place pecans in a 3½- or 4-quart slow cooker. In a small bowl combine butter, soy sauce, five-spice powder, garlic powder, ginger, and cayenne pepper. Pour butter mixture over nuts in cooker; stir to coat.

2. Cover and cook on low-heat setting for 2 hours.

3. Stir nuts. Spread nuts in a single layer on waxed paper to cool. (Nuts will appear soft after cooking but will crisp upon cooling.) Store in a tightly covered container for up to 2 weeks. **Makes 16 servings.**

PER SERVING: 216 cal., 23 g fat (4 g sat. fat), 8 mg chol., 141 mg sodium, 4 g carb., 3 g fiber, 3 g pro.

cook smart If you prefer, use whole almonds or walnut halves in place of the pecans. Any way you crack it, you'll be getting heart-healthy fats and a good dose of fiber.

● GLUTEN FREE

The smoky flavor of bourbon complements the sweet-tart flavor of citrus infused with aromatic spices such as cinnamon, cloves, and anise in this warming drink. (Pictured on page 49.)

bourbon-citrus sipper

PREP: 5 minutes **SLOW COOK:** 3½ hours (low) or 2 hours (high) + 30 minutes

6	cups apple cider or apple juice (48 ounces)
¼	cup sugar
9	inches stick cinnamon
8	whole cloves
½	teaspoon anise seeds
1	large navel orange, sliced
1	medium lemon, sliced
½	cup bourbon

1. In a 3- or 3½-quart slow cooker combine apple cider, sugar, cinnamon, cloves, and anise seeds.

2. Cover and cook on low-heat setting for 3½ to 4 hours or on high-heat setting for 2 hours. Add orange and lemon slices. Cover and cook for 30 minutes more.

3. Place a fine-mesh sieve over a large bowl; strain cider mixture. (Or use a slotted spoon to remove orange slices, lemon slice, and whole spices.) If using high-heat setting, turn cooker to low-heat setting. Pour the strained mixture back into the slow cooker to keep warm.

4. Just before serving, add bourbon to cider mixture. **Makes 8 servings.**

PER SERVING: 138 cal., 0 g fat, 0 mg chol., 1 mg sodium, 11 g carb., 1 g fiber, 0 g pro.

On a cool fall night, this beautiful ruby-red tea spiked with red wine will warm you up from head to toe. Pomegranate is high in antioxidants and may improve blood flow to the heart.

steaming pomegranate-ginger tea

PREP: 10 minutes   **SLOW COOK:** 5 hours (low) or 3 hours (high)   **STAND:** 2 minutes

3 cups pomegranate juice
3 cups water
2 cups apple cider or apple juice
1½ cups dry red wine
½ cup sugar
2 2-inch pieces fresh ginger, peeled
3 inches stick cinnamon
3 herbal tea bags, such as Red Zinger, or regular tea bags

1. In a 5- to 6-quart slow cooker combine pomegranate juice, the water, apple cider, wine, sugar, ginger, and cinnamon.

2. Cover and cook on low-heat setting for 5 to 5½ hours or on high-heat setting for 3 hours. Turn off cooker. Add tea bags; let stand for 2 minutes.* Remove and discard tea bags. **Makes 10 servings.**

*****Tip:** Leaving the tea bags in the slow cooker longer than 2 minutes will cause the drink to be bitter.

PER SERVING: 131 cal., 0 g fat, 0 mg chol., 8 mg sodium, 22 g carb., 0 g fiber, 0 g pro.

With a to-go mug of this authentic Indian-style tea in hand, you can drive right by the coffeehouse on your morning trek to work. It's delicious either hot or iced.

chai tea base

PREP: 15 minutes   **STAND:** 10 minutes   **SLOW COOK:** 6 hours (low) or 3 hours (high)

8	cups water
⅔	cup honey
4	2- to 3-inch sticks cinnamon
2	inches fresh ginger, thinly sliced
½	teaspoon whole cardamom seeds (without pods)
16	whole cloves
16	whole black peppercorns
¼	teaspoon ground nutmeg
12	black tea bags
7	cups low-fat milk

1. In a 3½- or 4-quart slow cooker stir together the water and honey until dissolved. Add stick cinnamon, ginger, cardamom seeds, cloves, peppercorns, and nutmeg.

2. Cover and cook on low-heat setting for 6 to 8 hours or on high-heat setting for 3 to 4 hours. Add tea bags. Cover and let stand 10 minutes. Strain the mixture through a fine-mesh sieve lined with a double thickness of 100-percent-cotton cheesecloth. Store in the refrigerator for up to 2 weeks.

3. For each serving, use ½ cup Chai Tea Base and ½ cup low-fat milk. Heat in a saucepan until steaming. **Makes 14 servings.**

Iced Chai: Prepare as directed, except serve over ice.

PER SERVING: 104 cal., 1 g fat (1 g sat. fat), 6 mg chol., 59 mg sodium, 20 g carb., 0 g fiber, 4 g pro.

 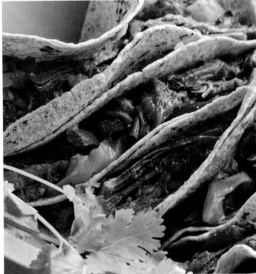 

beef

These meaty dishes capture a world of flavors—from Cajun to curry
to American classics such as pepper steak and sloppy joes.

Serve this New Orleans-style dish with a little jazz music and a bottle of hot pepper sauce for those who like to bump up the heat.

cajun beef roast

PREP: 25 minutes   **SLOW COOK:** 8 hours (low) or 4 hours (high)

1   2- to 2½-pound boneless beef chuck pot roast
1   tablespoon Cajun seasoning
1   14½-ounce can diced tomatoes
½   cup lower-sodium beef broth
1   medium red or yellow sweet pepper, cut in bite-size pieces
1   medium onion, cut in thin wedges
1   stalk celery, sliced
2   tablespoons quick-cooking tapioca, crushed
1   tablespoon Creole or horseradish mustard
1   fresh jalapeño or serrano chile pepper, seeded and minced (see tip, page 14)
3   cloves garlic, minced
½   teaspoon salt
3   cups hot cooked brown rice

1. Trim fat from meat. Sprinkle Cajun seasoning on meat, rubbing in with your fingers. If necessary, cut meat to fit into a 3½- or 4-quart slow cooker. In a large bowl combine undrained tomatoes, beef broth, sweet pepper, onion, celery, tapioca, mustard, jalapeño pepper, garlic, and salt. Pour over the meat.

2. Cover and cook on low-heat setting for 8 to 10 hours or on high-heat setting for 4 to 5 hours. Serve over hot brown rice. **Makes 6 servings.**

PER SERVING: 354 cal., 7 g fat (3 g sat. fat), 98 mg chol., 612 mg sodium, 32 g carb., 3 g fiber, 38 g pro.

BEEF

The process of drying fruit concentrates many of its nutrients—particularly fiber, iron, and vitamin A. This smoky-sweet pot roast is a great way to get more of those nutrients in a very tasty way.

pot roast with fruit and chipotle sauce

PREP: 15 minutes **SLOW COOK:** 10 hours (low) or 5 hours (high)

1 3-pound boneless beef chuck pot roast
2 teaspoons garlic-pepper seasoning
1 7-ounce package dried mixed fruit
½ cup water
1 tablespoon finely chopped chipotle peppers in adobo sauce (see tip, page 14)
1 tablespoon cold water
2 teaspoons cornstarch
Fresh cilantro sprigs (optional)

1. Trim fat from meat. If necessary, cut meat to fit into a 3½- or 4-quart slow cooker. Sprinkle both sides of meat with garlic-pepper seasoning. Place meat in cooker. Add fruit, the ½ cup water, and the chipotle peppers.

2. Cover and cook on low-heat setting for 10 to 11 hours or on high-heat setting for 5 to 5½ hours. Transfer meat and fruit to a serving platter; thinly slice meat. Cover meat and fruit and keep warm.

3. For sauce, pour cooking liquid into a bowl or glass measuring cup; skim off fat. In a medium saucepan combine the 1 tablespoon cold water and cornstarch; stir into cooking liquid. Cook and stir over medium heat until thickened and bubbly. Cook and stir for 2 minutes more.

4. Serve meat and fruit with sauce. If desired, garnish with cilantro. **Makes 8 servings.**

PER SERVING: 275 cal., 6 g fat (2 g sat. fat), 101 mg chol., 378 mg sodium, 17 g carb., 1 g fiber, 37 g pro.

cook smart Beef chuck may look like an unhealthful choice, but trim away the visible fat and this oh-so-tender cut of beef is actually quite lean when cooked. Three ounces of cooked beef chuck has just 182 calories and 6 grams of fat. Plus, it's high in satiating protein and provides a good dose of iron, which can help boost energy levels.

This super-tender beef has a subtle south-of-the-border accent from chili powder and the corn and pepper couscous. A squeeze of fresh lime brightens the flavor.

bbq beef roast with corn and pepper couscous

PREP: 25 minutes **SLOW COOK:** 10 hours (low) or 5 hours (high)

1	2- to 2½-pound boneless beef chuck pot roast
1	teaspoon chili powder
1	teaspoon ground cumin
½	teaspoon garlic salt
½	teaspoon ground black pepper
1	ounce can diced tomatoes with garlic and onion, undrained
¼	cup packed brown sugar
2	tablespoons vinegar
2	tablespoons Worcestershire sauce
1	tablespoon quick-cooking tapioca, crushed
½	teaspoon dry mustard
1	recipe Corn and Pepper Couscous Lime wedges (optional)

1. Trim fat from meat. In a small bowl stir together chili powder, cumin, garlic salt, and pepper. Sprinkle mixture evenly over meat; rub mixture in with your fingers. If necessary, cut meat to fit into a 3½- or 4-quart slow cooker. Place meat in cooker.

2. In a medium bowl combine tomatoes, brown sugar, vinegar, Worcestershire sauce, tapioca, and mustard. Pour over meat in cooker.

3. Cover and cook on low-heat setting for 10 to 11 hours or on high-heat setting for 5 to 5½ hours.

4. Transfer roast to a cutting board, reserving cooking liquid. Cut meat into pieces.

5. Serve meat with Corn and Pepper Couscous. Drizzle cooking liquid over meat and pass the remaining. If desired, serve with lime wedges. **Makes 8 servings.**

Corn and Pepper Couscous: In a small saucepan bring 1½ cups reduced-sodium chicken broth, ⅔ cup frozen whole kernel corn, ⅓ cup chopped red sweet pepper, and 1 tablespoon finely chopped fresh jalapeño chile pepper (see tip, page 14) to boiling. Add 1 cup whole wheat couscous. Remove from heat. Cover and let stand for 5 minutes. Fluff before serving. Sprinkle with 2 tablespoons snipped fresh cilantro.

PER SERVING: 371 cal., 14 g fat (5 g sat. fat), 56 mg chol., 520 mg sodium, 38 g carb., 4 g fiber, 23 g pro.

Comforting, creamy polenta is the perfect side for sopping up the delicious sauce from the roast. Be sure to stir regularly while cooking it to prevent it from splattering or sticking to the bottom of the pan.

balsamic beef roast with polenta

PREP: 30 minutes **SLOW COOK:** 8 hours (low) or 4 hours (high)

1   2- to 2½-pound boneless beef chuck pot roast
1   16-ounce package frozen small whole onions
¼   teaspoon salt
¼   teaspoon ground black pepper
1   cup lower-sodium beef broth
3   tablespoons balsamic vinegar
2   tablespoons tomato paste
2   tablespoons quick-cooking tapioca
3   cloves garlic, minced
1   teaspoon dried Italian seasoning, crushed
1   recipe Soft Polenta
    Snipped fresh Italian (flat-leaf) parsley
    Shaved Parmesan cheese (optional)

1. Trim fat from meat. If necessary, cut meat to fit into a 3½- or 4-quart slow cooker. Place frozen onions in cooker. Place meat on top of onions. Sprinkle meat with salt and pepper. In a small bowl combine the broth, vinegar, tomato paste, tapioca, garlic, and Italian seasoning. Pour mixture over meat.

2. Cover and cook on low-heat setting for 8 to 10 hours or on high-heat setting for 4 to 5 hours.

3. Transfer meat to a serving platter. Skim off fat from cooking liquid. Serve meat with Soft Polenta and cooking liquid. Sprinkle with parsley. If desired, garnish with cheese. **Makes 6 servings.**

Soft Polenta: In a medium saucepan bring 2¾ cups water to boiling. Meanwhile, in a medium bowl stir together 1 cup yellow cornmeal, 1 cup cold water, and ½ teaspoon salt. Slowly add cornmeal mixture to boiling water, stirring constantly. Cook and stir until mixture returns to boiling. Reduce heat to medium-low. Cook for 10 to 15 minutes or until mixture is very thick and tender, stirring frequently and adjusting heat as needed to maintain a slow boil. Makes 6 servings.

PER SERVING: 399 cal., 18 g fat (7 g sat. fat), 75 mg chol., 498 mg sodium, 31 g carb., 3 g fiber, 26 g pro.

cook smart Although the main benefit of onions may seem to be the flavor they impart, they are also quite healthful. They are high in quercetin, a powerful flavanoid that can help eliminate free radicals and protect against heart disease, and all for very few calories and virtually no sodium or fat.

BEEF

Any kind of dark beer works in this French dip-style sandwich—even a nonalcoholic variety.

shaved stein beef dip sandwiches

PREP: 30 minutes   **SLOW COOK:** 8 hours (low) or 4 hours (high)

Nonstick cooking spray
1   teaspoon canola oil
1½ pounds extra-lean boneless beef arm roast, trimmed of fat
1   tablespoon salt-free steak grilling blend
1   tablespoon reduced-sodium beef bouillon granules (3 packets)
2   teaspoons sugar
2   teaspoons instant espresso coffee powder
¼   teaspoon crushed red pepper
2   cups chopped onions (2 large)
1   12-ounce bottle dark beer
2   tablespoons balsamic vinegar
2   tablespoons steak sauce
8   whole grain hoagie rolls or sub rolls, warmed

1. Lightly coat a 3½- or 4-quart slow cooker with cooking spray.

2. In a large nonstick skillet heat oil over medium-high heat. Add meat; cook about 6 minutes or until brown on both sides, turning once.

3. Meanwhile, stir together steak grilling blend, bouillon granules, sugar, coffee powder, and crushed red pepper.

4. Place the onions in prepared slow cooker; top with meat. Pour beer and vinegar over meat and onions. Sprinkle with the steak grilling blend mixture.

5. Cover and cook on low-heat setting for 8 hours or on high-setting for 4 hours or until easily shredded.

6. Transfer meat to a cutting board, reserving cooking liquid in cooker. Using two forks, pull meat apart into shreds. Stir steak sauce into cooking liquid.

7. To serve, divide meat mixture among rolls; spoon some of the cooking liquid over shredded meat. Serve the remaining cooking liquid in small dishes. **Makes 8 servings.**

PER SERVING: 366 cal., 7 g fat (2 g sat. fat), 37 mg chol., 735 mg sodium, 46 g carb., 7 g fiber, 27 g pro.

cook smart Espresso doesn't have to be reserved for your double-shot latte. For virtually no calories, adding espresso powder to a spice rub for beef will add oomph to the flavor of the beef as well as the cooking liquid used for dipping the sandwiches.

You can serve this stew with regular brown rice, but the nutty flavor and enticing aroma of basmati rice measurably enhances the enjoyment of it.

beef curry

PREP: 25 minutes   **SLOW COOK:** 8 hours (low) or 4 hours (high)

3   cups fresh cauliflower florets

2   medium carrots, peeled and cut into 1-inch pieces

1   medium onion, cut in thin wedges

1   fresh serrano chile pepper, seeded and finely chopped (see tip, page 14)

2   pounds boneless beef shank, cut into 1½-inch pieces

1   14½-ounce can no-salt-added diced tomatoes, undrained

3   tablespoons red curry paste

1   tablespoon grated fresh ginger

¼   teaspoon salt

3   cups fresh baby spinach

1   cup unsweetened light coconut milk

3   cups hot cooked brown basmati rice

1. In a 3½- or 4-quart slow cooker combine cauliflower, carrots, onion, and serrano pepper. Top with beef. In a medium bowl combine tomatoes, curry paste, ginger, and salt. Pour over all.

2. Cover and cook on low-heat setting for 8 hours or on high-heat setting for 4 hours. Stir in spinach and coconut milk. Serve over brown basmati rice. **Makes 6 servings.**

PER SERVING: 381 cal., 8 g fat (3 g sat. fat), 58 mg chol., 788 mg sodium, 38 g carb., 6 g fiber, 39 g pro.

A trio of sweet peppers—red, green, and yellow—contributes to the full serving of vegetables contained in a single serving of these beefy fajitas.

slow-cooked beef fajitas

PREP: 25 minutes   **SLOW COOK:** 8 hours (low) or 4 hours (high)

1½   pounds beef flank steak
1   large green sweet pepper, cored, seeded, and cut into ½-inch-wide slices
1   large red sweet pepper, cored, seeded, and cut into ½-inch-wide slices
1   large yellow sweet pepper, cored, seeded, and cut into ½-inch-wide slices
1   large onion, sliced
1   16-ounce jar salsa verde (about 1¾ cups)
8   8-inch whole wheat flour tortillas, warmed*
½   cup light sour cream

1. Trim fat from meat. If necessary, cut meat to fit into a 3½- or 4-quart slow cooker. Place peppers and onion into cooker. Top with meat. Pour salsa over meat.

2. Cover and cook on low-heat setting for 8 to 10 hours or on high-heat setting for 4 to 5 hours. Transfer meat to a cutting board; use two forks to pull meat apart into shreds.

3. Using a slotted spoon remove peppers and onion from cooker. If desired, drizzle meat with a little cooking liquid.

4. Spoon some of the meat and vegetables onto one side of each warmed tortilla; top with sour cream. Fold tortilla in half over filling. **Makes 8 servings.**

*****Tip:** To warm tortillas, preheat oven to 350°F. Stack tortillas and wrap tightly in foil. Heat about 10 minutes or until heated through.

PER SERVING: 327 cal., 9 g fat (4 g sat. fat), 37 mg chol., 657 mg sodium, 37 g carb., 4 g fiber, 23 g pro.

cook smart Fajitas make one of the healthiest meals you can order at a Mexican restaurant, and the great thing is that they are a cinch to make at home. This recipe uses three colors of sweet peppers, which contain a lot of immune-boosting vitamin C. A half cup of cooked peppers provides 116 mg vitamin C, which is over 1½ times the level found in a medium orange.

Switch up the flavor of this family favorite depending on the flavor of the stewed tomatoes you use—Cajun, Mexican, and Italian all work equally well.

so-easy pepper steak

PREP: 15 minutes   **SLOW COOK:** 9 hours (low) or 4½ hours (high)

2 pounds boneless beef round steak, cut ¾ to 1 inch thick

½ teaspoon salt

¼ teaspoon ground black pepper

1 14½-ounce can Cajun-, Mexican-, or Italian-style stewed tomatoes, undrained

½ of a 6-ounce can (⅓ cup) tomato paste

½ teaspoon bottled hot pepper sauce (optional)

1 16-ounce package frozen yellow, green, and red peppers and onions stir-fry vegetables

4 cups hot cooked whole wheat pasta (optional)

1. Trim fat from meat. Cut meat into six serving-size portions. Sprinkle meat with salt and black pepper. Place meat in a 3½- or 4-quart slow cooker.

2. In a medium bowl combine tomatoes, tomato paste, and, if desired, hot pepper sauce. Pour over meat in cooker. Top with frozen vegetables.

3. Cover and cook on low-heat setting for 9 to 10 hours or on high-heat setting for 4½ to 5 hours.

4. If desired, serve over hot cooked pasta. **Makes 6 servings.**

PER SERVING: 258 cal., 6 g fat (2 g sat. fat), 83 mg chol., 644 mg sodium, 12 g carb., 2 g fiber, 37 g pro.

This French-style dish made with white wine and Dijon mustard is elegant enough for entertaining on a night when you're pressed for time. Serve it with French-cut green beans for a fresh touch.

dijon beef and mushrooms

PREP: 25 minutes   **SLOW COOK:** 8 hours (low) or 4 hours (high) + 30 minutes (high)

1½ pounds boneless beef sirloin steak, cut into 1-inch pieces
½ teaspoon salt
¼ teaspoon ground black pepper
2 8-ounce packages button and/or cremini mushrooms, quartered
1 cup chopped onion (1 large)
3 cloves garlic, minced
⅔ cup lower-sodium beef broth
⅔ cup dry white wine
3 tablespoons Dijon style mustard
1 tablespoon snipped fresh thyme or 1 teaspoon dried thyme, crushed
1 tablespoon butter, softened
1 tablespoon all-purpose flour
1 recipe Whole Wheat Bread Planks

1. Sprinkle meat with salt and pepper. If desired, in a large nonstick skillet cook and stir half of the meat over medium-high heat until brown. Drain off fat. Place meat in a 3½- or 4-quart slow cooker. Repeat with remaining meat.

2. Add mushrooms, onion, and garlic to cooker. In a bowl stir together broth, wine, mustard, and dried thyme (if using). Pour mixture over meat in cooker.

3. Cover and cook on low-heat setting for 8 to 10 hours or on high-heat setting for 4 to 5 hours.

4. If using low-heat setting, turn cooker to high-heat setting. In a small bowl stir together butter and flour. Stir in 2 tablespoons cooking liquid to make a paste. Stir in fresh thyme if using. Stir mixture into slow cooker. Cover and cook on high-heat setting about 30 minutes more or until mixture thickens.

5. Serve meat mixture with Whole Wheat Bread Planks. Sprinkle with fresh thyme. **Makes 6 servings.**

Whole Wheat Bread Planks: Preheat broiler. Diagonally cut six 1-inch-thick slices from a loaf of whole wheat baguette-style French bread. Lightly brush some of 2 teaspoons olive oil over one side of each bread slice. Rub the cut side of a garlic clove over the oil-brushed side of each slice. Place slices on a baking sheet. Broil 4 to 5 inches from heat for 1 to 2 minutes or until toasted. Carefully watch the bread because it can burn easily. Makes 6 planks.

PER SERVING: 343 cal., 11 g fat (4 g sat. fat), 66 mg chol., 681 mg sodium, 23 g carb., 4 g fiber, 33 g pro.

The gremolata—an aromatic mixture of fresh basil, Parmesan cheese, and garlic—adds a touch of freshness and bright flavor to this veggie-rich dish.

mediterranean beef with pasta

PREP: 25 minutes   **SLOW COOK:** 7 hours (low) or 3½ hours (high) + 30 minutes (high)

1	tablespoon olive oil
1½	pounds lean beef stew meat, cut into 1-inch pieces and trimmed of fat
3	medium carrots, cut into ½-inch slices
1	medium onion, cut into thin wedges
1	medium yellow sweet pepper, cut into 1-inch pieces
1	teaspoon dried Italian seasoning, crushed
2	cloves garlic, minced
¼	teaspoon salt
¼	teaspoon ground black pepper
1	14½-ounce can diced tomatoes, undrained
½	cup lower-sodium beef broth
1	medium zucchini, halved lengthwise and cut into ¼-inch-thick slices
6	ounces dried multigrain or whole grain penne pasta
1	recipe Basil Gremolata

1. In a large skillet heat oil over medium-high heat. Add half of the meat; cook and stir until brown. Place meat in a 3½- or 4-quart slow cooker. Repeat with remaining meat. Add carrots, onion, and sweet pepper to cooker. Sprinkle with Italian seasoning, garlic, salt, and black pepper. Pour tomatoes and broth over meat and vegetables in cooker.

2. Cover and cook on low-heat setting for 7 to 9 hours or on high-heat setting for 3½ to 4½ hours.

3. If using low-heat setting, turn to high-heat setting. Stir in zucchini. Cover and cook for 30 minutes more. Meanwhile, cook pasta according to package directions; drain.

4. Serve meat and vegetable mixture over pasta. Sprinkle with Basil Gremolata. **Makes 6 servings.**

Basil Gremolata: In a small bowl stir together 2 tablespoons snipped fresh basil, 2 tablespoons finely shredded Parmesan cheese, and 2 cloves garlic, minced. Makes about ⅓ cup.

PER SERVING: 354 cal., 11 g fat (4 g sat. fat), 62 mg chol., 403 mg sodium, 31 g carb., 5 g fiber, 32 g pro.

Wheat berries can be cooked in bulk for other uses. In a 4-quart slow cooker combine 2 cups wheat berries and 6⅔ cups water. Cook 4½ hours on low. You'll get 5 cups (drained) cooked wheat berries.

sweet-and-sour meatballs and beets with wheat berries

PREP: 25 minutes   **SLOW COOK:** 5 hours (high)

1	cup wheat berries, rinsed
1	14½-ounce can reduced-sodium chicken broth
1¼	cups water
2	tablespoons molasses or honey
2	tablespoons stone-ground mustard
¼	teaspoon salt
4	cups red onions, thinly sliced (2 medium)
1	pound fresh beets, peeled and cut into wedges
¾	cup snipped dried apricots
2	tablespoons quick-cooking rolled oats
2	tablespoons fat-free milk
1	tablespoon finely chopped red onion
1	tablespoon snipped fresh parsley
1	teaspoon Worcestershire sauce
½	teaspoon freshly ground black pepper
1	clove garlic, minced
12	ounces lean ground beef
3	tablespoons red wine vinegar
	Light sour cream (optional)
	Snipped fresh parsley (optional)

1. Place wheat berries in a 4- to 5-quart slow cooker. In a medium bowl whisk together broth, the water, molasses, mustard, and salt; pour into slow cooker. Add the sliced red onions, beets, and apricots.

2. Cover and cook on high-heat setting about 3 hours or until wheat berries are tender but still chewy.

3. Meanwhile, in a medium bowl combine oats, milk, the finely chopped onion, the 1 tablespoon parsley, the Worcestershire sauce, pepper, and garlic; gently mix in ground beef. Using a teaspoon, shape meat mixture into 24 small meatballs. Stir meatballs into mixture in cooker

4. Cover and cook for 2 hours more. Stir in vinegar.

5. If desired, top each serving with sour cream and sprinkle with additional parsley. **Makes 8 servings.**

PER SERVING: 249 cal., 5 g fat (2 g sat. fat), 28 mg chol., 372 mg sodium, 38 g carb., 6 g fiber, 14 g pro.

Smoked paprika adds a distinctive flavor to these tacos. For a milder flavor, simply omit it or reduce the amount to 1 teaspoon.

soft-style beef tacos

PREP: 20 minutes **SLOW COOK:** 5 hours (low) or 2½ hours (high)

Nonstick cooking spray
1 pound extra-lean ground beef
1 15-ounce can no-salt-added (or reduced-sodium) black beans, rinsed and drained
1½ cups chopped onions (3 medium)
1 10-ounce can diced tomatoes and green chiles
1 1¼-ounce package 40-percent-less-sodium taco seasoning mix
1 tablespoon smoked paprika, (optional)
2 teaspoons sugar
1½ teaspoons ground cumin
10 low-carb or whole wheat flour tortillas, warmed (see tip, page 70)
Lime wedges
Fat-free sour cream (optional)
Snipped fresh cilantro (optional)
Finely chopped red onion (optional)
Shredded romaine lettuce (optional)

1. Coat a large nonstick skillet with cooking spray. Heat over medium-high heat. Add ground beef; cook until brown, using a wooden spoon to break up meat as it cooks.

2. Coat a 3½- or 4-quart slow cooker with cooking spray. In prepared cooker combine ground beef, beans, the 1½ cups chopped onions, the tomatoes and green chiles, taco seasoning mix, paprika (if desired), sugar, and cumin.

3. Cover and cook on low-heat setting for 5 hours or on high-heat setting for 2½ hours.

4. Spoon ground beef* mixture into tortillas. Serve with lime wedges and, if desired, sour cream, cilantro, the red onion, and lettuce. **Makes 10 servings.**

*Tip: Place any leftovers in an airtight container and freeze for up to 1 month.

PER SERVING: 206 cal., 4 g fat (1 g sat. fat), 28 mg chol., 594 mg sodium, 26 g carb., 11 g fiber, 16 g pro.

cook smart These tacos are loaded with fiber, thanks to the black beans and low-carb tortillas, which tend to be much higher in fiber than regular whole wheat flour tortillas. Compared to a fast-food taco, one Soft-Style Beef Taco has nearly four times as much fiber. That's worth skipping the drive-thru.

BEEF

Savory with a hint of sweetness from raisins and cinnamon—and a bit of heat from jalapeño, these sandwiches don't skimp on flavor.

picadillo-style beef pockets

PREP: 20 minutes   **SLOW COOK:** 6 hours (low) or 3 hours (high)

Nonstick cooking spray
1 pound extra-lean ground beef
1 14½-ounce can diced tomatoes, drained
1 cup chopped onion (1 large)
½ cup chopped green sweet pepper (1 small)
1 fresh jalapeño chile pepper, thinly sliced and, if desired, seeded (see tip, page 14)
⅓ cup raisins
2 cloves garlic, minced
1 bay leaf
½ teaspoon dried thyme, crushed
½ teaspoon ground cinnamon
½ teaspoon roasted ground cumin or ground cumin
¼ teaspoon ground nutmeg
⅛ teaspoon ground allspice
2 ounces slivered almonds, toasted (see tip, page 23)
½ teaspoon salt
4 whole wheat pita bread rounds, halved and warmed*
8 Bibb lettuce leaves
½ cup plain fat-free yogurt

1. Coat a large nonstick skillet with cooking spray. Add ground beef; cook until brown, using a wooden spoon to break up meat as it cooks.

2. Coat a 3- or 3½-quart slow cooker with cooking spray. Place the beef in cooker; stir in tomatoes, onion, sweet pepper, jalapeño pepper, raisins, garlic, bay leaf, thyme, cinnamon, cumin, nutmeg, and allspice.

3. Cover and cook on low-heat setting for 6 to 7 hours or on high-heat setting for 3 to 3½ hours Remove and discard bay leaf. Stir in the almonds and salt.

4. Line the inside of each pita bread round half with a lettuce leaf. Spoon beef mixture into the pita bread halves; top beef mixture in each pita half with yogurt. **Makes 8 servings.**

*Tip: To warm pita bread halves, preheat oven to 350°F. Wrap pita bread tightly in foil; heat about 10 minutes or until heated through.

PER SERVING: 255 cal., 7 g fat (2 g sat. fat), 35 mg chol., 457 mg sodium, 30 g carb., 5 g fiber, 19 g pro.

Fresh mushrooms, shredded carrots, and finely chopped sweet peppers bulk up the filling for these popular sandwiches and give them a nutritional boost.

spicy beef sloppy joes

PREP: 20 minutes   **SLOW COOK:** 8 hours (low) or 4 hours (high)

2   pounds lean ground beef
2   16-ounce jars salsa
3   cups sliced fresh mushrooms (8 ounces)
1½   cups shredded carrots (3 medium)
1½   cups finely chopped red and/or green sweet peppers (2 medium)
⅓   cup tomato paste
2   teaspoons dried basil, crushed
4   cloves garlic, minced
1   teaspoon dried oregano, crushed
½   teaspoon salt
¼   teaspoon cayenne pepper
18   kaiser rolls, split and toasted

1. In a large skillet cook ground beef over medium heat until brown, using a wooden spoon to break up meat as it cooks. Drain off fat. In a 5- to 6-quart slow cooker combine meat, salsa, mushrooms, carrots, sweet peppers, tomato paste, basil, garlic, oregano, salt, and the cayenne pepper.

2. Cover and cook on low-heat setting for 8 to 10 hours or on high-heat setting for 4 to 5 hours.

3. Serve meat mixture in kaiser rolls.* **Makes 18 servings.**

***Tip:** If you like, use only one-third (enough for 6 servings) of the meat mixture now and store the rest for later in two 6-serving-size portions. Place one-third of the meat mixture into each of two airtight containers. Seal, label, and freeze for up to 3 months. Thaw overnight in refrigerator before using.

PER SERVING: 268 cal., 5 g fat (2 g sat. fat), 31 mg chol., 691 mg sodium, 36 g carb., 3 g fiber, 18 g pro.

BEEF

These Greek-style sandwiches are so good, you might think they came from your favorite gyro stand. The meat has the authentic taste and firm texture of traditional gyro meat, but it is much more healthful.

beef gyros

PREP: 25 minutes   **SLOW COOK:** 4 hours (low) or 2 hours (high)   **STAND:** 10 minutes

1   large sweet onion, cut into thin wedges
2   pounds extra-lean ground beef
2   teaspoons dried oregano, crushed
3   cloves garlic, minced
½   teaspoon salt
½   teaspoon ground black pepper
½   teaspoon paprika
6   oval whole wheat wraps
3   roma tomatoes, sliced
⅓   cup crumbled reduced-fat feta cheese
1   recipe Tzatziki Sauce

1. In a 3½- or 4-quart slow cooker place onion. In a large bowl combine beef, oregano, garlic, salt, pepper, and paprika.

2. On waxed paper, shape meat mixture into a 5-inch round loaf. Crisscross three 18×2-inch foil strips. Place meat loaf in center of strips. Bringing up foil strips, lift and transfer meat and foil to the slow cooker over the onion. Press the meat away from the side of slow cooker to avoid burning.

3. Cover and cook on low-heat setting for 4 to 5 hours or on high-heat setting for 2 to 2½ hours.

4. Using foil strips, carefully lift meat loaf from the slow cooker and transfer to a cutting board. Let stand for 10 minutes before thinly slicing.*

5. Divide sliced meat and onion among whole wheat wraps. Top with tomatoes, feta cheese, and Tzatziki Sauce. **Makes 6 servings.**

Tzatziki Sauce: In a medium bowl stir together one 6-ounce carton plain Greek yogurt; 1 cup shredded, seeded cucumber; 1 tablespoon lemon juice; 1 tablespoon snipped fresh dill weed; 1 teaspoon honey; 1 clove minced garlic; and ¼ teaspoon salt. Serve immediately or cover and chill for up to 4 hours.

*Tip: Cut the loaf in half crosswise, then place, cut sides down, on the cutting board for easiest slicing.

PER SERVING: 386 cal., 11 g fat (4 g sat. fat), 97 mg chol., 820 mg sodium, 32 g carb., 8 g fiber, 45 g pro.

These hearty sandwiches are extra saucy and require a knife and fork—so you know they will be good!

open-face shredded beef sandwiches

PREP: 25 minutes   **SLOW COOK:** 9 hours (low) or 4½ hours (high)

- 1 tablespoon instant espresso coffee granules
- 1 pound extra-lean boneless chuck roast, trimmed of fat
- Nonstick cooking spray
- 1½ cups chopped onions (3 medium)
- ½ of a medium red sweet pepper, cut into thin bite-size strips
- ½ of a medium green sweet pepper, cut into thin bite-size trips
- 4 cloves garlic, minced*
- 2 dried bay leaves
- ½ cup dry red wine
- 2 tablespoons cider vinegar
- 1 tablespoon Worcestershire sauce
- ½ teaspoon salt
- 6 thick slices multigrain Italian bread (about 1½ ounces each)
- 6 thin slices provolone cheese (3 ounces total)

1. Press the coffee granules into both sides of roast. Coat a medium nonstick skillet with cooking spray; heat over medium-high heat. Add roast; cook until light brown on both sides, turning once.

2. Meanwhile, coat a 3- or 3½-quart slow cooker with cooking spray. Layer onions, pepper strips, garlic, and bay leaves in cooker. If necessary, cut roast to fit into cooker. Place roast on top of vegetables.

3. Add wine to skillet; bring to boiling over medium-high heat, scraping brown bits from bottom and sides of skillet. Remove from heat; stir in vinegar and Worcestershire sauce. Pour over roast.

4. Cover and cook on low-heat setting for 9 to 10 hours or on high-heat setting for 4½ to 5 hours.

5. Using a slotted spoon, transfer meat to a cutting board. Remove and discard bay leaves. Add salt to mixture in cooker. Using two forks, pull meat apart into shreds; return to cooker, stirring to combine.

6. Preheat broiler. Arrange bread slices on a baking sheet; top each with a cheese slice. Broil 4 to 5 inches from heat until cheese melts and bread is toasted.

7. To serve, using a slotted spoon, divide meat mixture among bread slices. **Makes 6 servings.**

*****Tip:** Each clove of minced garlic is about ½ teaspoon. You may substitute 2 teaspoons minced garlic from a jar for the 4 cloves of fresh garlic.

PER SERVING: 272 cal., 8 g fat (4 g sat. fat), 31 mg chol., 563 mg sodium, 26 g carb., 4 g fiber, 21 g pro.

The last-minute addition of shredded fresh spinach gives this favorite soup of savory meatballs and orzo pasta an eye-catching splash of green—as well as big doses of vitamins K, A, and C and folate.

italian wedding soup

PREP: 35 minutes   **SLOW COOK:** 8 hours (low) or 4 hours (high) + 20 minutes (high)

1	large onion
1	egg, lightly beaten
3	oil-packed dried tomatoes, drained and finely snipped
¼	cup fine dry bread crumbs
2	teaspoons dried Italian seasoning, crushed
1	pound lean ground beef
2	teaspoons olive oil
1	fennel bulb
2	14½-ounce cans reduced-sodium chicken broth
3½	cups water
6	cloves garlic, thinly sliced
½	teaspoon ground black pepper
¾	cup dried orzo pasta (rosamarina)
5	cups shredded fresh spinach

1. Finely chop one-third of the onion; thinly slice the remaining onion. In a large bowl combine chopped onion, egg, dried tomatoes, bread crumbs, and 1 teaspoon of the Italian seasoning. Add ground beef; mix well. Shape into 12 meatballs. In a large skillet cook meatballs in hot oil over medium-high heat until brown on all sides. Carefully drain off fat. Transfer meatballs to a 4½- or 5-quart slow cooker.

2. Meanwhile, cut off and discard upper stalks of fennel. If desired, reserve some of the feathery leaves for garnish. Remove any wilted outer layers; cut off a thin slice from fennel base. Cut fennel into thin wedges; add to cooker. Add sliced onion, the remaining 1 teaspoon Italian seasoning, broth, the water, garlic, and pepper.

3. Cover and cook on low-heat setting for 8 to 10 hours or on high-heat setting for 4 to 5 hours.

4. If using low-heat setting, turn to high-heat setting. Gently stir in uncooked pasta. Cover and cook for 20 to 30 minutes more or until pasta is tender.

5. Stir in spinach. If desired, garnish each serving with the reserved fennel leaves. **Makes 6 servings.**

PER SERVING: 283 cal., 10 g fat (3 g sat. fat), 83 mg chol., 515 mg sodium, 26 g carb., 3 g fiber, 21 g pro.

Kale is a potent source of vitamins A, C, and K and is also high in fiber. Incorporating it into this flavorful soup makes eating your greens an exercise in enjoyment.

kale, beef, and white bean stew

PREP: 25 minutes   **SLOW COOK:** 6 hours (low) or 3 hours (high) + 30 minutes (high)

1¼ pounds boneless beef top sirloin steak, cut into 1-inch cubes

1 cup chopped onion (1 large)

1 14½-ounce can stewed tomatoes, undrained

1 14½-ounce can lower-sodium beef broth

1 tablespoon sweet Hungarian paprika or paprika

1 teaspoon dried thyme, crushed

2 cloves garlic, minced

½ teaspoon dried rosemary, crushed

¼ teaspoon ground black pepper

7 cups fresh kale, rinsed, trimmed, and chopped (about 1 bunch)

2 15-ounce cans no-salt-added cannellini beans, drained and rinsed

1 to 2 tablespoons balsamic vinegar

1. In a 4- to 5-quart slow cooker stir together beef, onion, tomatoes, broth, paprika, thyme, garlic, rosemary, and pepper.

2. Cover and cook on low-heat setting for 6 to 7 hours or on high-heat setting for 3 to 3½ hours.

3. If using low-heat setting, turn cooker to high-heat setting. Stir in kale and beans. Cover and cook for 30 minutes more.

4. To serve, stir in vinegar. **Makes 6 servings.**

PER SERVING: 326 cal., 7 g fat (2 g sat. fat), 29 mg chol., 562 mg sodium, 39 g carb., 9 g fiber, 30 g pro.

The bright and beautiful vegetables in this traditional beef stew boost its appeal. Reduced-fat buttermilk biscuits make a perfect accompaniment.

hearty vegetable beef stew

PREP: 30 minutes   **SLOW COOK:** 8 hours (low) or 4 hours (high) + 30 minutes (high)

Nonstick cooking spray
2   pounds boneless beef chuck roast, cut into 1-inch cubes
12   ounces tiny new potatoes, quartered
4   medium carrots, cut into ½-inch pieces
1   medium onion, cut into wedges
1   10¾-ounce can reduced-fat and reduced-sodium condensed cream of mushroom soup
1   cup lower-sodium beef broth
1   teaspoon dried marjoram or dried thyme, crushed
2   cups frozen cut green beans

1. Coat a large skillet with cooking spray; heat over medium-high heat. Add half of the beef cubes. Cook and stir until brown; remove from skillet. Add remaining beef cubes; cook and stir until brown. Drain off fat.

2. Place meat in a 3½- or 4-quart slow cooker. Add potatoes, carrots, onion, cream of mushroom soup, broth, and marjoram. Stir to combine.

3. Cover and cook on low-heat setting for 8 to 9 hours or on high-heat setting for 4 to 4½ hours.

4. If using low-heat setting, turn cooker to high-heat setting. Stir in green beans. Cover and cook about 30 minutes more or just until beans are tender. **Makes 6 servings.**

PER SERVING: 317 cal., 9 g fat (3 g sat. fat), 92 mg chol., 396 mg sodium, 22 g carb., 4 g fiber, 35 g pro.

Ancho chile has a mildly spicy, fruity flavor. If you don't have concerns about gluten, serve this simple stew with warm corn bread.

ancho beef stew

PREP: 15 minutes   **SLOW COOK:** 8 hours (low) or 4 hours (high)

1	**pound boneless beef chuck roast**
1	**tablespoon ground ancho chile pepper**
	Nonstick cooking spray
1	**16-ounce package frozen stew vegetables**
1	**cup frozen whole kernel corn**
1	**16-ounce jar salsa**
½	**cup water**

1. Trim fat from meat. Cut meat into 1-inch pieces. Sprinkle meat with ancho chile pepper, tossing to coat all sides. Lightly coat a large skillet with cooking spray; heat skillet over medium-high heat. Cook meat, half at a time, in hot skillet until brown.

2. In a 3½- or 4-quart slow cooker combine frozen stew vegetables and frozen corn. Add meat. Pour salsa and the water over mixture in cooker.

3. Cover and cook on low-heat setting for 8 to 9 hours or on high-heat setting for 4 to 4½ hours. **Makes 4 servings.**

PER SERVING: 272 cal., 5 g fat (1 g sat. fat), 50 mg chol., 84 mg sodium, 28 g carb., 5 g fiber, 30 g pro.

cook smart Frozen vegetables are just as nutritious as fresh vegetables because they are picked at the peak of ripeness and quickly frozen to lock in nutrients. They make a great addition to a quick weeknight slow cooker meal.

BEEF

If your supermarket carries extra-lean stew meat, use it in this tantalizing stew to cut the fat even more.

barley-beef soup

PREP: 25 minutes   **SLOW COOK:** 8 hours (low) or 4 hours (high)

12	ounces beef or lamb stew meat
1	tablespoon vegetable oil
4	14½-ounce cans lower-sodium beef broth
1	14½-ounce can diced tomatoes, undrained
1	cup chopped onion (1 large)
1	cup peeled parsnip or potato cut into ½-inch pieces
1	cup frozen mixed vegetables
⅔	cup regular barley
½	cup chopped celery (1 stalk)
1	bay leaf
2	cloves garlic, minced
1	teaspoon dried oregano or basil, crushed
¼	teaspoon ground black pepper

1. Trim fat from meat. Cut meat into 1-inch pieces. In a large skillet cook meat in hot oil over medium-high heat until brown. Drain off fat.

2. Transfer meat to a 5- or 6-quart slow cooker. Stir in broth, tomatoes, onion, parsnip, frozen vegetables, barley, celery, bay leaf, garlic, oregano, and pepper.

3. Cover and cook on low-heat setting for 8 to 10 hours or on high-heat setting for 4 to 5 hours. Remove bay leaf and discard before serving. **Makes 8 servings.**

PER SERVING: 168 cal., 4 g fat (1 g sat. fat), 25 mg chol., 492 mg sodium, 20 g carb., 3 g fiber, 13 g pro.

pork & lamb

Chops, roasts, stew meats—even sausages—simmer with veggies
and spices to savory goodness in these satisfying meat dishes.

Poblano chile peppers give this pork dish heat. To reduce the heat, remove the seeds and membranes from inside the pepper. If you like it hot, leave them in.

spiced pork with squash and potatoes

PREP: 40 minutes   **SLOW COOK:** 7 hours (low) or 3 hours (high)

1	pound butternut squash, halved, seeded, peeled, and cut into 1-inch cubes
1	pound sweet potatoes, peeled and cut into 1-inch cubes
1	tablespoon olive oil
¼	cup packed brown sugar
1	teaspoon salt
1	teaspoon ground cumin
½	teaspoon ground black pepper
½	teaspoon ground cinnamon
½	teaspoon ground ginger
2	fresh poblano peppers, seeded and cut into bite-size strips (see tip, page 14)
2	small onions, cut into thin wedges
1	2- to 2½-pound pork shoulder roast, trimmed of fat and cut into 1-inch cubes
⅔	cup reduced-sodium chicken broth
1	tablespoon snipped fresh parsley

1. In a large bowl combine squash and sweet potatoes. Drizzle oil over vegetables, tossing to coat. In a small bowl combine brown sugar, salt, cumin, black pepper, cinnamon, and ginger. Add half of the spice mixture to squash mixture; set remainder aside. Toss squash mixture to coat pieces. Transfer to a 4½- or 5-quart slow cooker. Add poblano peppers and onions to cooker.

2. In the same bowl combine the meat and the remaining spice mixture, tossing to coat pieces. Add meat to cooker. Pour broth over meat.

3. Cover and cook on low-heat setting for 7 to 8 hours or on high-heat setting for 3 to 3½ hours.

4. To serve, transfer squash mixture and meat to a serving bowl. Sprinkle with parsley. **Makes 4 servings.**

PER SERVING: 453 cal., 11 g fat (3 g sat. fat), 82 mg chol., 858 mg sodium, 58 g carb., 7 g fiber, 30 g pro.

Serve whole grain noodles or brown rice with the fragrant apple-spice sauce and super tender meat—and maybe some applesauce on the side.

pork roast and harvest vegetables

PREP: 30 minutes   **SLOW COOK:** 10 hours (low) or 5 hours (high)

1	1½- to 2-pound boneless pork shoulder roast
1	tablespoon vegetable oil
2	cups parsnips cut into ½-inch pieces (3 medium)
1½	cups carrots cut into ½-inch pieces (3 medium)
1	large green sweet pepper, cut into bite-size pieces
1	cup celery cut into ½-inch pieces (2 stalks)
3	tablespoons quick-cooking tapioca
1	6-ounce can frozen apple juice concentrate, thawed
¼	cup water
1	teaspoon instant beef bouillon granules
¼	teaspoon ground cinnamon
¼	teaspoon ground black pepper

1. Trim fat from meat. If necessary, cut meat to fit into a 3½- to 5-quart slow cooker. In a large skillet heat oil over medium heat; add meat. Cook meat until brown, turning to brown evenly on all sides. In the cooker combine parsnips, carrots, sweet pepper, and celery. Sprinkle with the tapioca.

2. In a small bowl combine apple juice concentrate, the water, bouillon granules, cinnamon, and black pepper. Pour over vegetables. Place meat on top of vegetables.

3. Cover and cook on low-heat setting for 10 to 12 hours or on high-heat setting for 5 to 6 hours.

4. Transfer meat and vegetables to a serving platter. Strain cooking liquid; skim off fat. Drizzle some of the cooking liquid over meat; pass remaining cooking liquid. **Makes 6 servings.**

PER SERVING: 309 cal., 9 g fat (3 g sat. fat), 73 mg chol., 272 mg sodium, 32 g carb., 4 g fiber, 24 g pro.

The sassiness in this dish comes from a spike of smoky chipotle chiles in adobo sauce. The recipe calls for 1 tablespoon. Freeze any remaining chiles and sauce in 1- to 2-tablespoon portions in small freezer bags.

sassy pork chops

PREP: 25 minutes   **SLOW COOK:** 6 hours (low) or 3 hours (high)

2   medium red, green, and/or yellow sweet peppers, cut into strips
1   cup thinly sliced celery (2 stalks)
½   cup chopped onion (1 medium)
8   pork loin chops (with bone), cut ¾ inch thick
½   teaspoon garlic salt
¼   teaspoon ground black pepper
2   tablespoons vegetable oil
¼   cup reduced-sodium chicken broth
¼   cup orange juice
1   tablespoon chopped chipotle chile peppers in adobo sauce (see tip, page 14)
½   teaspoon dried oregano, crushed

1. In a 4- to 5-quart slow cooker layer sweet peppers, celery, and onion; set aside. Season chops with garlic salt and black pepper. In a very large skillet heat oil over medium heat. Cook chops, half at a time, until brown on both sides. Add chops to cooker. In a small bowl combine broth, orange juice, chipotle peppers, and oregano. Pour over chops in cooker.

2. Cover and cook on low-heat setting for 6 to 7 hours or on high-heat setting for 3 to 3½ hours.

3. Using a slotted spoon, transfer chops and vegetables to a serving platter; discard cooking liquid. **Makes 8 servings.**

PER SERVING: 215 cal., 7 g fat (1 g sat. fat), 78 mg chol., 363 mg sodium, 4 g carb., 1 g fiber, 33 g pro.

Chipotle peppers are smoked jalapeños, so they offer considerable heat as well as a subtle smokiness. The adobo sauce contains more chiles, as well as herbs and vinegar.

cranberry-chipotle country-style ribs

PREP: 15 minutes   **SLOW COOK:** 7 hours (low) or 3½ hours (high)

2½ to 3 pounds boneless pork
   country-style ribs
   Salt
   Ground black pepper
1 16-ounce can whole cranberry
   sauce
1 cup chopped onion (1 large)
3 chipotle peppers in adobo sauce,
   finely chopped (see tip, page 14)
1½ teaspoons bottled minced garlic
   (3 cloves)

1. Trim fat from ribs. Sprinkle ribs with salt and black pepper. Place ribs in a 3½- or 4-quart slow cooker. For sauce, in a medium bowl combine cranberry sauce, onion, chipotle peppers, and garlic. Pour the sauce over the ribs.

2. Cover and cook on low-heat setting for 7 to 8 hours or on high-heat setting for 3½ to 4 hours.

3. Transfer ribs to a serving platter. Stir sauce. Drizzle some of the sauce over ribs. If desired, serve with the remaining sauce. **Makes 6 servings.**

PER SERVING: 395 cal., 10 g fat (4 g sat. fat), 139 mg chol., 247 mg sodium, 32 g carb., 2 g fiber, 40 g pro.

● LOW CALORIE ◉ HIGH FIBER ● GLUTEN FREE

Stuffed cabbage rolls manage to be homey and special at the same time. All this Eastern European-style dish needs to go with it is some rye rolls or crusty bread.

pork stuffed cabbage rolls

PREP: 1 hour 15 minutes **SLOW COOK:** 6½ hours (low) or 3½ hours (high)

1	3-pound green cabbage, cored
1	pound ground pork
1½	cups cooked brown rice
½	cup chopped onions
½	cup golden raisins
3	tablespoons canned tomato paste
4	cloves garlic, minced
1	teaspoon salt
½	teaspoon ground black pepper
½	teaspoon caraway seeds, crushed
1	14½-ounce can no-salt-added diced tomatoes
1	8-ounce can low-sodium vegetable juice
1	8-ounce can tomato sauce
2	tablespoons reduced-sodium Worcestershire sauce
2	teaspoons packed brown sugar

1. Bring a large pot of lightly salted water to a boil. Boil cabbage 12 to 15 minutes, carefully removing 16 leaves with long-handled tongs as they become pliable. Drain well, then remove tough stems from leaves. Remove remaining cabbage from water and shred 4 cups (discard any remaining cabbage). Place shredded cabbage in bottom of a 5- to 6-quart slow cooker.

2. In a large bowl combine the pork, rice, onions, raisins, tomato paste, garlic, ½ teaspoon of the salt, ¼ teaspoon of the pepper, and the caraway. Evenly divide the pork mixture among the 16 cabbage leaves, using a scant ⅓ cup per leaf. Fold sides of leaf over filling and roll up.

3. In a medium bowl combine the tomatoes, vegetable juice, tomato sauce, Worcestershire sauce, brown sugar, remaining ½ teaspoon salt, and remaining ¼ teaspoon pepper. Pour half of the tomato mixture over shredded cabbage in cooker. Stir to mix. Place cabbage rolls on the shredded cabbage. Top with remaining tomato mixture.

4. Cover and cook on low-heat setting for 6½ to 7½ hours or on high-heat setting for 3½ to 4 hours (a cabbage roll in center of cooker should register 160°F on an instant-read thermometer). Carefully remove the cooked cabbage rolls and serve with the shredded cabbage. **Makes 8 servings.**

PER SERVING: 280 cal., 10 g fat (3 g sat. fat), 39 mg chol., 634 mg sodium, 36 g carb., 7 g fiber, 15 g pro.

If you can't find uncooked pork and chicken sausages, you can use fully cooked Italian-style chicken sausage links. They generally come in 12-ounce packages of 4 links. Use 6 sausages to have enough.

mediterreanean-style sausage and peppers pita

PREP: 20 minutes   **SLOW COOK:** 5 hours (low) or 2½ hours (high)

1   17-ounce package reduced-fat uncooked pork and chicken mild Italian sausage links (5 links)
1   14½-ounce can no-salt-added diced tomatoes
1½   cups sliced onion
2   red sweet peppers, cut into bite-size strips
1   green sweet pepper, cut into bite-size strips
½   cup sliced Kalamata olives
1   tablespoon snipped fresh oregano
2   cloves garlic, minced
¼   teaspoon ground black pepper
5   pita bread rounds, halved
1   medium cucumber, sliced
⅔   cup reduced-fat crumbled feta cheese

1. In a 3½- or 4-quart slow cooker combine the sausage, tomatoes, onion, red peppers, green pepper, olives, oregano, garlic, and ground black pepper. Cover and cook on low-heat setting for 5 to 6 hours or on high-heat setting for 2½ to 3 hours.

2. Transfer sausage links from slow cooker to a cutting board. When cool enough to handle, cut sausage in half lengthwise and crosswise.

3. To assemble, place two sausage pieces into a pita bread half. Use a slotted spoon to spoon onion and pepper mixture over the sausage. Top with slices of cucumber and feta cheese. **Makes 10 servings.**

PER SERVING: 245 cal., 10 g fat (3 g sat. fat), 35 mg chol., 701 mg sodium, 27 g carb., 3 g fiber, 14 g pro.

Traditional French cassoulet is a dish of white beans simmered with a variety of meats (including sausages and duck leg preserved in its own fat). This hearty version is decidedly more healthful.

pork-lentil cassoulet

PREP: 20 minutes   **SLOW COOK:** 10 hours (low) or 4½ hours (high)

12	ounces boneless pork shoulder roast
1	onion, cut into wedges
2	cloves garlic, minced
2	teaspoons vegetable oil
2½	cups water
4	medium carrots and/or parsnips, peeled and cut into ½-inch slices
1	14½-ounce can diced tomatoes, undrained
1	cup thinly sliced celery (2 stalks)
¾	cup brown lentils, rinsed and drained
1½	teaspoons dried rosemary, crushed
1	teaspoon instant beef bouillon granules
¼	teaspoon salt
¼	teaspoon ground black pepper
	Fresh rosemary sprigs (optional)

1. Trim fat from meat. Cut meat into ¾-inch pieces. In a large nonstick skillet cook meat, onion, and garlic in hot oil over medium-high heat until meat is brown. Drain off fat.

2. Transfer meat mixture to a 3½- or 4-quart slow cooker. Stir in the water, carrots and/or parsnips, undrained tomatoes, celery, lentils, dried rosemary, bouillon granules, salt, and pepper.

3. Cover and cook on low-heat setting for 10 to 12 hours or on high-heat setting for 4½ to 5½ hours. If desired, garnish each serving with fresh rosemary. **Makes 4 servings.**

PER SERVING: 354 cal., 12 g fat (3 g sat. fat), 37 mg chol., 641 mg sodium, 37 g carb., 5 g fiber, 26 g pro.

cook smart Adding a lot of vegetables, dry beans, and lentils to a slow cooker meal allows you to stretch the amount of meat and still get a generous serving of the main dish. You'll save fat and calories by eating a smaller portion of meat and get the bonus of eating plenty of nutrient-dense vegetables and beans.

Just a little bit of smoky ham gives this broth-based soup great flavor; wild rice gives it a nutty flavor and hearty texture.

wild rice-ham soup

PREP: 20 minutes   **SLOW COOK:** 6 hours (low) or 3 hours (high) + 30 minutes (high)

5	cups water
1	14½-ounce can reduced-sodium chicken broth
1	cup chopped celery (2 stalks)
1	cup diced cooked ham (about 5 ounces)
¾	cup uncooked wild rice, rinsed and drained
1	medium onion, cut into thin wedges
1½	teaspoons dried thyme, crushed
1½	cups chopped red sweet peppers (2 medium)
4	cups shredded fresh spinach

1. In a 4- to 5-quart slow cooker combine the water, broth, celery, ham, uncooked wild rice, onion, and thyme.

2. Cover and cook on low-heat setting for 6 to 7 hours or on high-heat setting for 3 to 3½ hours.

3. If using low-heat setting, turn to high-heat setting. Stir in sweet peppers. Cover and cook for 30 minutes more. Stir in spinach. **Makes 6 servings.**

PER SERVING: 124 cal., 1 g fat (0 g sat. fat), 11 mg chol., 584 mg sodium, 20 g carb., 3 g fiber, 10 g pro.

Hominy offers a pleasing chewiness and flavor that complements the green chiles and tomatillos in the salsa verde in this New Mexican favorite. Serve with whole grain or corn tortillas.

green chile-pork posole

PREP: 25 minutes   **SLOW COOK:** 6 hours (low) or 3 hours (high)

2   15½-ounce cans hominy, rinsed and drained
1   16-ounce jar salsa verde
1   14½-ounce can reduced-sodium chicken broth
2   4-ounce cans diced green chiles, undrained
1   cup coarsely chopped onion (1 large)
1   tablespoon ground cumin
4   cloves garlic, minced
1   teaspoon dried oregano, crushed
¼   teaspoon crushed red pepper
12 ounces pork tenderloin, cut into ½-inch cubes
    Snipped fresh cilantro
6   to 7 whole grain tortillas, warmed (see tip, page 70)

1. In a 3½- or 4-quart slow cooker combine hominy, salsa, broth, chiles, onion, cumin, garlic, oregano, and crushed red pepper. Stir in meat.

2. Cover and cook on low-heat setting for 6 to 7 hours or on high-heat setting for 3 to 3½ hours.

3. To serve, sprinkle each serving with cilantro. Serve with tortillas. **Makes 6 servings.**

PER SERVING: 271 cal., 6 g fat (1 g sat. fat), 37 mg chol., 784 mg sodium, 40 g carb., 13 g fiber, 22 g pro.

This easy-to-prep Mexican-style soup is packed with flavor and comforting ingredients.

red posole

PREP: 20 minutes   **SLOW COOK:** 8 hours (low) or 4 hours (high) + 30 minutes (high)

1½ pounds boneless pork shoulder, cut into 1-inch cubes

2 15-ounce cans hominy, rinsed and drained

1 cup chopped onion (1 large)

1 4-ounce can diced green chiles, undrained

1 tablespoon ancho chile powder

1½ teaspoons dried oregano, crushed

2 cloves garlic, minced

½ teaspoon ground cumin

2 14½-ounce cans reduced-sodium chicken broth

2 cups coarsely chopped cabbage

1 10-ounce can enchilada sauce
   Lime wedges
   Fresh pineapple wedges (optional)

1. In a 4- to 5-quart slow cooker combine pork, hominy, onion, green chiles, chile powder, oregano, garlic, and cumin. Pour broth over mixture in cooker.

2. Cover and cook on low-heat setting for 8 to 9 hours or on high-heat setting for 4 to 4½ hours.

3. If using low-heat setting, turn to high-heat setting. Stir in cabbage and enchilada sauce. Cover and cook for 30 minutes more.

4. To serve, garnish with lime wedges and, if desired, pineapple wedges. **Makes 8 servings.**

PER SERVING: 279 cal., 12 g fat (4 g sat. fat), 53 mg chol., 659 mg sodium, 23 g carb., 4 g fiber, 19 g pro.

● LOW CALORIE

This soup requires a little more effort than some throw-and-go slow cooker recipes, but the fabulously flavorful and aromatic result is well worth it.

thai bbq pork soup

PREP: 30 minutes   **MARINATE:** 4 hours   **SLOW COOK:** 8 hours (low) or 4 hours (high) + 30 minutes (high)

1¼   cups unsweetened light coconut milk
2   tablespoons reduced-sodium soy sauce
2   tablespoons finely chopped fresh lemongrass
2   tablespoons packed brown sugar
2   tablespoons red curry paste
1   tablespoon fish sauce
4   cloves garlic, minced
1   2- to 2½-pound boneless pork shoulder roast, trimmed of fat and cut into 1-inch pieces
2   tablespoons canola oil
2   14½-ounce cans reduced-sodium chicken broth
1   14-ounce can whole baby corn, drained and cut into 1-inch pieces
8   ounces button mushrooms, quartered
½   cup chopped onion
1   red sweet pepper, cut into bite-size strips
2   fresh serrano chile peppers, seeded and thinly sliced (see tip, page 14) (optional)
2   tablespoons lime juice
2   teaspoons grated fresh ginger
½   cup basil leaves, coarsely snipped

1. In a medium bowl combine ¼ cup of the coconut milk, the soy sauce, lemongrass, brown sugar, curry paste, fish sauce, and garlic. Place the pork in a large resealable plastic bag. Pour coconut milk mixture over the pork. Seal bag and place in a shallow dish. Marinate in the refrigerator for 4 to 24 hours.

2. Remove pork from marinade; reserve marinade. In a very large skillet heat oil over medium-high heat. Add pork and cook 3 minutes on each side or until brown. Drain fat. Transfer pork to a 5- to 6-quart slow cooker. Pour reserved marinade over pork. Add chicken broth, baby corn, mushrooms, and onion. Cover and cook on low-heat setting for 8 to 9 hours or on high-heat setting for 4 to 4½ hours.

3. Stir in the remaining coconut milk, the red sweet pepper, serrano peppers (if using), lime juice, and ginger. If using low-heat setting, turn to high-heat setting. Cover and cook for 30 minutes more. Skim fat from the top of the soup. Garnish with snipped basil leaves. **Makes 8 servings.**

PER SERVING: 209 cal., 10 g fat (4 g sat. fat), 46 mg chol., 876 mg sodium, 11 g carb., 2 g fiber, 19 g pro.

This twist on traditional wild rice soup is simple to prep for the slow cooker and is a hearty, flavorful dinner for any night of the week.

italian wild rice soup

PREP: 25 minutes   **SLOW COOK:** 7 hours (low) or 3½ hours (high)

1	pound ground pork
4	cups water
2	14½-ounce cans reduced-sodium beef broth
1	14½-ounce can no-salt-added diced tomatoes with basil, garlic, and oregano, undrained
1	6-ounce can tomato paste
1	cup chopped onion (1 large)
¾	cup wild rice, rinsed and drained
6	cloves garlic, minced
2	tablespoons Italian seasoning, crushed
1½	teaspoons paprika
1	teaspoon fennel seeds
½	teaspoon ground black pepper
¼	teaspoon salt
¼	teaspoon crushed red pepper
1	9-ounce package fresh spinach, chopped
½	cup finely shredded Parmesan cheese (2 ounces)

1. In a large skillet cook pork over medium heat until no longer pink, using a wooden spoon to break up meat as it cooks; drain off fat.

2. In a 4- to 6-quart slow cooker combine cooked pork, the water, broth, tomatoes, tomato paste, onion, uncooked wild rice, garlic, Italian seasoning, paprika, fennel seeds, black pepper, salt, and crushed red pepper.

3. Cover and cook on low-heat setting for 7 to 8 hours or on high-heat setting for 3½ to 4 hours. Stir spinach into soup.

4. Serve topped with cheese. **Makes 8 servings.**

PER SERVING: 272 cal., 11 g fat (5 g sat. fat), 45 mg chol., 632 mg sodium, 24 g carb., 6 g fiber, 20 g pro.

● LOW CALORIE ● GLUTEN FREE

Place small bowls of the toppers—steamed broccoli florets, shredded cheddar, and fresh thyme—on the table so everyone can customize his or her meal.

creamy ham and potato chowder

PREP: 20 minutes **SLOW COOK:** 3½ hours (high)

12	ounces tiny yellow potatoes, cut into ¾-inch pieces
1	cup chopped onion (1 large)
2	14½-ounce cans reduced-sodium chicken broth
¼	cup cornstarch
½	teaspoon dried thyme, crushed
¼	teaspoon ground black pepper
1	12-ounce can evaporated fat-free milk (1½ cups)
½	cup diced cooked lean ham
1	cup coarsely shredded carrots (2 medium)
1	cup broccoli florets, steamed
¼	cup shredded cheddar cheese (1 ounce)
2	teaspoons snipped fresh thyme

1. In a 4-quart slow cooker combine potatoes and onion. Pour broth over vegetables.

2. Cover and cook on high-heat setting for 3 hours.

3. In a medium bowl combine cornstarch, dried thyme, and pepper. Whisk in evaporated milk. Slowly stir the cornstarch mixture, ham, and carrots into the hot soup. Cover and cook for 30 minutes more, stirring the soup occasionally.

4. Serve soup topped with broccoli, cheese, and fresh thyme. **Makes 6 servings.**

PER SERVING: 171 cal., 2 g fat (1 g sat. fat), 12 mg chol., 566 mg sodium, 27 g carb., 3 g fiber, 11 g pro.

This dish has the tantalizing qualities of beef stroganoff—meat and mushrooms in a creamy sherry sauce served over noodles—but features flavorful lamb sirloin instead.

lamb stroganoff

PREP: 25 minutes   **SLOW COOK:** 6 hours (low) or 3 hours (high) + 30 minutes (high)

1¾	pounds boneless lamb sirloin or leg, cut into 1-inch pieces
1	tablespoon olive oil
¾	cup 50%-reduced-sodium beef broth
4	cups sliced fresh button mushrooms
2	cups sliced onions
1	tablespoon Dijon mustard
3	cloves garlic, minced
1	bay leaf
½	teaspoon salt
¼	teaspoon ground black pepper
1	8-ounce carton light sour cream
⅓	cup all-purpose flour
¼	cup dry sherry
¼	cup snipped fresh Italian (flat-leaf) parsley
1	12-ounce package dried whole grain wide noodles, cooked according to package directions

1. Trim fat from meat. In a very large skillet brown the lamb in hot oil over medium-high heat. Drain off fat.

2. In a 3½- or 4-quart slow cooker combine the lamb, broth, mushrooms, onions, mustard, garlic, bay leaf, salt, and pepper. Cover and cook on low-heat setting for 6 to 8 hours or on high-heat setting for 3 to 4 hours.

3. In a medium bowl whisk together sour cream, flour, and sherry until smooth. Stir about ½ cup of the hot liquid into sour cream mixture. Return all to cooker; stir to combine. Cover and cook on high-heat setting for 30 minutes or until thickened and bubbly. Remove and discard bay leaf. Stir in parsley. Serve over noodles. **Makes 8 servings.**

PER SERVING: 373 cal., 10 g fat (3 g sat. fat), 74 mg chol., 325 mg sodium, 40 g carb., 5 g fiber, 31 g pro.

This rich and elegant special-occasion dish is perfect for a holiday dinner. While it simmers and fills the house with wonderful aromas, you can attend to other things.

lamb with fig and pomegranate sauce

PREP: 30 minutes **COOK:** 10 minutes **SLOW COOK:** 9 hours (low) or 4½ hours (high)

1	4- to 4½-pound boneless lamb shoulder roast, trimmed of fat
2	tablespoons snipped fresh rosemary
2	tablespoons snipped fresh thyme
2	cloves garlic, minced
1	teaspoon salt
½	teaspoon ground black pepper
1¼	cups pomegranate juice
1	cup dried figs, stems removed and halved
½	cup fig preserves
1	tablespoon cornstarch
¼	cup snipped fresh Italian (flat-leaf) parsley
1	teaspoon finely shredded orange peel
1	clove garlic, minced

1. Trim fat from meat. If necessary cut meat to fit into a 4- to 5-quart slow cooker. In a small bowl combine the rosemary, thyme, garlic, salt, and pepper. Rub herb mixture onto outside of lamb. Place lamb into the slow cooker.

2. In a medium bowl combine 1 cup of the pomegranate juice, the dried figs, and preserves. Pour around roast in the slow cooker. Cover and cook on low-heat setting for 9 to 10 hours or on high-heat setting for 4½ to 5 hours.

3. Transfer meat to a serving platter; cover and keep warm. Meanwhile, for sauce, pour cooking liquid into a bowl or glass measuring cup; skim off fat. In a medium saucepan combine remaining ¼ cup pomegranate juice and cornstarch; stir in cooking liquid. Cook and stir over medium heat until thickened and bubbly. Cook and stir for 2 minutes more.

4. In a small bowl combine the parsley, orange peel, and garlic. Sprinkle parsley mixture on top of lamb. Slice lamb and serve with fig and pomegranate sauce. **Makes 10 servings.**

PER SERVING: 256 cal., 7 g fat (2 g sat. fat), 72 mg chol., 321 mg sodium, 26 g carb., 2 g fiber, 22 g pro.

cook smart Rich-tasting, succulent lamb is actually a great choice when you're trying to eat healthfully. When trimmed of fat and cooked, lamb shoulder meat is lower in calories and fat than cooked beef chuck and pork shoulder.

Fiber-rich lentils and oats bulk up this homey meat loaf. Leftovers are delicious the next day warmed up or sliced thin and eaten cold on a sandwich with a little light mayo.

lamb and lentil meat loaf

PREP: 25 minutes   **SLOW COOK:** 3½ hours (low) or 2½ hours (high) + 30 minutes (high)   **STAND:** 15 minutes

2	pounds lean ground lamb
1	cup refrigerated steamed lentils
3	eggs, lightly beaten
¾	cup rolled oats
½	cup milk
½	cup finely chopped onion
½	cup finely chopped celery
2	tablespoons snipped fresh Italian (flat-leaf) parsley
1	tablespoon snipped fresh sage
¾	teaspoon salt
½	teaspoon ground black pepper
½	cup reduced-sugar ketchup
2	tablespoons reduced-sodium Worcestershire sauce
1	tablespoon stone-ground mustard
1	tablespoon cider vinegar

1. In a very large bowl combine the lamb, lentils, eggs, oats, milk, onions, celery, parsley, sage, salt, and pepper. Mix well.

2. Cut three 18×3-inch heavy foil strips. Crisscross the strips in a 6-quart oval or round slow cooker. Place meat mixture on top of strips in the cooker. Shape meat mixture into an oval or round loaf shape depending on the shape of cooker being used. Press meat mixture away from sides of cooker to avoid burning.

3. Cover and cook on low-heat setting for 3½ to 4 hours or on high-heat setting for 2½ to 3 hours. If using low-heat setting, turn to high-heat setting. In a small bowl combine the ketchup, Worcestershire sauce, mustard, and vinegar. Spoon ketchup mixture over meat loaf. Cover and cook 30 minutes more.

4. Using foil strips, carefully lift meat loaf from the slow cooker and transfer to a serving plate. Let stand for 15 minutes before slicing. **Makes 12 servings.**

PER SERVING: 244 cal., 13 g fat (5 g sat. fat), 97 mg chol., 402 mg sodium, 12 g carb., 3 g fiber, 18 g pro.

The exotic aromas of a North African spice market fill the kitchen as this dish cooks. For even more flavor, add ¼ to ½ teaspoon ground turmeric when preparing the couscous.

moroccan-style lamb

PREP: 15 minutes **SLOW COOK:** 6 hours (low) or 3 hours (high)

2 pounds lean boneless lamb, cut into ¾-inch cubes
2 large onions, cut into wedges
2 large carrots, cut into 1-inch pieces
3 medium tomatoes, chopped
1 14½-ounce can chicken broth
1½ teaspoons ground cumin
½ teaspoon ground turmeric
¼ teaspoon crushed red pepper (optional)
1 10-ounce package whole wheat couscous (1½ cups)
¼ cup dried currants, raisins, or golden raisins
   Plain low-fat Greek yogurt (optional)
   Snipped fresh mint (optional)

1. In a 3½- or 4-quart slow cooker combine meat, onions, carrots, tomatoes, broth, cumin, turmeric, and, if desired, crushed red pepper.

2. Cover and cook on low-heat setting for 6 to 7 hours or on high-heat setting for 3 to 3½ hours.

3. Prepare couscous according to package directions, adding currants to the pan.

4. Using a slotted spoon, transfer meat mixture to a serving bowl; keep warm. Skim off fat from cooking liquid; pour skimmed cooking liquid over lamb mixture.

5. With a fork, fluff couscous mixture just before serving. Serve meat mixture with couscous mixture. If desired, top each serving with yogurt and mint. **Makes 8 servings.**

PER SERVING: 404 cal., 15 g fat (7 g sat. fat), 74 mg chol., 354 mg sodium, 40 g carb., 7 g fiber, 29 g pro.

cook smart Boneless lamb shoulder is a good option when a recipe calls for lean boneless lamb. It cooks beautifully in the slow cooker and results in tender, juicy meat.

Tapioca is an excellent thickener. The easiest way to crush it is with a mortar and pestle. If you don't have one, place the tapioca between layers of waxed paper and crush it with a rolling pin.

irish stew

PREP: 25 minutes   **SLOW COOK:** 10 hours (low) or 5 hours (high)

1	pound lean boneless lamb
2	tablespoons vegetable oil
2	medium turnips, peeled and cut into ½-inch pieces
3	medium carrots, cut into ½-inch pieces
2	medium potatoes, peeled and cut into ½-inch pieces
2	medium onions, cut into thin wedges
¼	cup quick-cooking tapioca, crushed
½	teaspoon salt
¼	teaspoon dried thyme, crushed
¼	teaspoon ground black pepper
2	14½-ounce cans beef broth

1. Trim fat from meat. Cut meat into 1-inch pieces. In a large skillet heat oil over medium-high heat. Cook half of the meat in hot oil until brown on all sides; remove from skillet. Repeat with the remaining meat. Drain off fat.

2. Transfer meat to a 3½- or 4-quart slow cooker. Stir in turnips, carrots, potatoes, onions, tapioca, salt, thyme, and pepper. Pour broth over mixture in cooker.

3. Cover and cook on low-heat setting for 10 to 11 hours or on high-heat setting for 5 to 5½ hours. **Makes 6 servings.**

PER SERVING: 234 cal., 8 g fat (2 g sat. fat), 49 mg chol., 784 mg sodium, 21 g carb., 3 g fiber, 19 g pro.

cook smart Turnips are underrated. They are a perfect match for the slow cooker and can be substituted for potatoes in many of your favorite slow cooker recipes. Compared to a medium potato, the same amount of turnip has less than half the calories and just as much fiber as the potato, making it an excellent choice when watching your waistline.

The sweetness of the sweet potato pairs perfectly with mild heat from the poblano chiles in this highly spiced chili. Serve it with extra hot sauce for those heat-seeking diners.

lamb, bean, and sweet potato chili

PREP: 25 minutes **SLOW COOK:** 7 hours (low) or 3½ hours (high)

1½	pounds lean boneless lamb, cut into 1-inch pieces
2	15-ounce cans no-salt-added black beans, rinsed and drained
2	14½-ounce cans no-salt-added diced tomatoes
1	14½-ounce can redcued-sodium beef broth
1	pound sweet potatoes, peeled and cut into 1-inch pieces (3 cups)
2	fresh poblano chile peppers, chopped (1½ cups) (see tip, page 14)
1	cup chopped onions
½	cup chopped carrots
½	cup chopped celery
1	teaspoon salt
1	teaspoon ground cumin
1	teaspoon dried oregano, crushed
1	teaspoon chili powder
½	teaspoon ground black pepper
1	to 2 tablespoons bottled Louisiana hot sauce Nonfat plain Greek yogurt (optional)

1. In a 5- to 6-quart slow cooker combine the lamb, beans, undrained tomatoes, broth, sweet potatoes, poblano peppers, onions, carrots, celery, salt, cumin, oregano, chili powder, and pepper.

2. Cover and cook on low-heat setting for 7 to 8 hours or on high-heat setting for 3½ to 4 hours. Stir in hot sauce. If desired, serve with yogurt. **Makes 8 servings.**

PER SERVING: 273 cal., 4 g fat (1 g sat. fat), 55 mg chol., 622 mg sodium, 35 g carb., 9 g fiber, 26 g pro.

cook smart Greek yogurt can be used as a topper for almost any recipe in place of sour cream. Swapping 2 tablespoons nonfat plain Greek yogurt for sour cream will save you about 20 calories and you'll get double the amount of calcium.

poultry

Make the most of lean chicken and turkey (without drying them out) and rediscover how to get healthful weeknight dinners on the table.

Two kinds of peppers, tomatoes, green olives, chili powder, cumin, and a squeeze of fresh lime give this simple-to-prep dish great Latin flavor.

cuban chicken

PREP: 25 minutes   **SLOW COOK:** 5 hours (low)

¾ cup chopped green sweet pepper (1 medium)
⅓ cup chopped onion (1 small)
1 fresh jalapeño chile pepper, stemmed, seeded, and finely chopped (see tip, page 14)
2½ pounds skinless, bone-in chicken breast halves
1 14½-ounce can diced tomatoes, undrained
1 cup frozen corn kernels
½ cup reduced-sodium chicken broth
¼ cup pitted green olives, sliced
2 tablespoons quick-cooking tapioca
2 teaspoons chili powder
2 cloves garlic, minced
½ teaspoon salt
½ teaspoon ground cumin
½ teaspoon ground black pepper
10 8-inch whole grain tortillas, warmed (see tip, page 70)
3½ cups hot cooked brown rice
1 lime, cut into wedges

1. In a 3½- or 4-quart slow cooker combine sweet pepper, onion, and jalapeño pepper. Add chicken. In a medium bowl stir together tomatoes, frozen corn, broth, olives, tapioca, chili powder, garlic, salt, cumin, and black pepper. Pour over chicken in cooker.

2. Cover and cook on low-heat setting for 5 to 6 hours. Transfer chicken to a cutting board, reserving cooking liquid in cooker. Remove meat from bones; discard bones. Using two forks, pull chicken apart into shreds. Return chicken to cooker, stirring to combine.

3. Using a slotted spoon, serve chicken mixture with tortillas, brown rice, and lime wedges. Drizzle chicken with some of the cooking liquid. **Makes 10 servings.**

PER SERVING: 333 cal., 6 g fat (1 g sat. fat), 43 mg chol., 709 mg sodium, 40 g carb., 13 g fiber, 28 g pro.

If you crave the hot wings at your local sports bar, this dish will hit the spot. This recipe is slimmed down and has some veggies and whole grains—but the familiar flavor is still the one you love.

buffalo chicken and rice

PREP: 15 minutes   **SLOW COOK:** 6 hours (low) or 3 hours (high) + 30 minutes

3 green onions
1¼ pounds boneless, skinless chicken breasts, cut into 1-inch cubes
1 cup very thinly sliced carrots (2 medium)
1 cup celery cut into ¼-inch pieces (2 stalks)
½ cup tomato sauce
½ cup reduced-sodium chicken broth
1 Anaheim pepper, cut into ¼-inch pieces (about ⅓ cup) (see tip, page 14)
1 1-ounce package ranch salad dressing mix
2 tablespoons hot pepper sauce
4 ounces reduced-fat cream cheese
3 cups hot cooked brown rice
¼ cup crumbled blue cheese (1 ounce)

1. Thinly slice green onions, separating white and green parts; set aside. In a 3-quart slow cooker combine chicken, carrots, celery, tomato sauce, broth, Anaheim pepper, salad dressing mix, the white parts of green onions, and the hot sauce.

2. Cover and cook on low-heat setting for 6 hours or on high-heat setting for 3 hours.

3. Stir in cream cheese and the green parts of green onions. Cover and cook for 30 minutes longer.

4. Serve chicken mixture over hot cooked rice; sprinkle with blue cheese. **Makes 6 servings.**

PER SERVING: 314 cal., 8 g fat (4 g sat. fat), 73 mg chol., 774 mg sodium, 30 g carb., 3 g fiber, 28 g pro.

If you're using the bacon in this creamy, saucy chicken dish, sprinkle it on just before serving so it stays nice and crisp.

jalapeño chicken breasts

PREP: 15 minutes   **SLOW COOK:** 5 hours (low) or 2½ hours (high) + 15 minutes (high)

6 bone-in chicken breast halves, skinned
1 tablespoon chili powder
⅛ teaspoon salt
½ cup reduced-sodium chicken broth
2 tablespoons lemon juice
⅓ cup sliced pickled jalapeño chile peppers, drained (see tip, page 14)
1 tablespoon cornstarch
1 tablespoon cold water
1 8-ounce package reduced-fat cream cheese (Neufchâtel), softened and cut into cubes
2 slices regular bacon or turkey bacon, crisp-cooked, drained, and crumbled (optional)

1. Sprinkle chicken with chili powder and salt. Arrange chicken, bone sides down, in a 4½- to 6-quart slow cooker. Pour broth and lemon juice around chicken. Top with jalapeño peppers.

2. Cover and cook on low-heat setting for 5 to 6 hours or on high-heat setting for 2½ to 3 hours.

3. Transfer chicken and jalapeño peppers to a serving platter, reserving cooking liquid. Cover chicken and keep warm.

4. If using low-heat setting, turn to high-heat setting. For sauce, in a small bowl combine cornstarch and the water; stir into cooking liquid. Add cream cheese, whisking until combined. Cover and cook about 15 minutes more or until thickened. Serve chicken with sauce. If desired, sprinkle with bacon. **Makes 6 servings.**

PER SERVING: 329 cal., 11 g fat (6 g sat. fat), 143 mg chol., 489 mg sodium, 5 g carb., 1 g fiber, 49 g pro.

Garam masala—an Indian spice blend of black pepper, cinnamon, cloves, coriander, cumin, cardamom, dried chiles, fennel, mace, and nutmeg—offers big flavor in a single teaspoon.

dried fruit, chicken, and bulgur pilaf

PREP: 20 minutes **SLOW COOK:** 2 hours (low)

2   teaspoons canola oil
1¼   pounds skinless, boneless chicken breast halves, cut into bite-size strips
½   cup coarsely chopped onion (1 medium)
1   teaspoon garam masala
1½   cups bulgur
½   of a medium lemon, seeded and thinly sliced
¾   cup pitted dried plums, quartered
⅓   cup golden raisins
½   teaspoon ground ginger
½   teaspoon ground cinnamon
¼   teaspoon ground allspice
     Pinch cayenne pepper
1   14½-ounce can reduced-sodium chicken broth
1¼   cups water
⅓   cup coarsely chopped or slivered almonds, toasted (see tip, page 23)
     Fresh mint leaves, thinly sliced
     Finely shredded lemon peel

1. In a large skillet heat oil over medium heat. Add chicken, onion, and garam masala; cook and stir until chicken is brown on all sides and onion is tender.

2. In a 3½- or 4-quart slow cooker combine the chicken mixture, bulgur, lemon slices, plums, raisins, ginger, cinnamon, allspice, and cayenne pepper. Pour broth and the water over mixture in cooker.

3. Cover and cook on low-heat setting for 2 hours. Stir in almonds.

4. To serve, sprinkle each serving with mint and lemon peel. **Makes 6 servings.**

PER SERVING: 321 cal., 6 g fat (1 g sat. fat), 55 mg chol., 235 mg sodium, 41 g carb., 9 g fiber, 29 g pro.

cook smart Bulgur is parboiled, dried, and cracked hard wheat that is a high-fiber choice as a base for salads and grain side dishes. It cooks quickly and can be found in most supermarkets.

Dried figs are potent providers of iron, folic acid, and potassium. You can use either Golden Calimyrna or dark purple Mission dried figs in this autumnal recipe.

figgy chicken and wild rice

PREP: 20 minutes   **SLOW COOK:** 3 hours (high)

¾   cup wild and whole grain rice blend, rinsed and drained, or ¼ cup wild rice and ½ cup brown rice

1   medium onion, halved and thinly sliced

4   small boneless chicken breast halves (about 1¼ pounds total)

½   teaspoon garlic pepper

1   14½-ounce can reduced-sodium chicken broth

¼   cup dry white wine or reduced-sodium chicken broth

1   teaspoon finely shredded orange peel

½   teaspoon ground black pepper

¼   teaspoon salt

1   cup coarsely chopped dried figs (6 ounces)

2   tablespoons snipped fresh parsley

1   medium orange, cut into wedges

1. In a 3½- or 4-quart slow cooker combine uncooked rice and onion. Top with chicken. Sprinkle chicken with garlic pepper. In medium bowl stir together broth, wine, orange peel, black pepper, and salt. Pour over mixture in cooker.

2. Cover and cook on high-heat setting for 2½ hours. Stir in figs. Cover and cook about 30 minutes more.

3. Serve chicken over rice mixture. Sprinkle with parsley. Serve with orange wedges. **Makes 4 servings.**

PER SERVING: 421 cal., 3 g fat (1 g sat. fat), 82 mg chol., 528 mg sodium, 58 g carb., 7 g fiber, 40 g pro.

An intriguing blend of spices makes this slow-simmer chicken and potato dish sizzle with flavors that are typical of Indian cuisine.

indian curry chicken

PREP: 25 minutes **SLOW COOK:** 8¼ hours (low) or 4¼ hours (high) + 15 minutes (high)

5	medium white potatoes (about 1½ pounds), peeled
1	medium green sweet pepper, seeded and cut into 1-inch pieces
1	medium onion, sliced
1	pound skinless, boneless chicken breast halves or thighs, cut into 1-inch pieces
1½	cups chopped tomatoes (3 medium)
1	tablespoon ground coriander
1½	teaspoons paprika
1	teaspoon grated fresh ginger or ¼ teaspoon ground ginger
¾	teaspoon salt
½	teaspoon ground turmeric
¼	to ½ teaspoon crushed red pepper
¼	teaspoon ground cinnamon
⅛	teaspoon ground cloves
1	cup chicken broth
2	tablespoons cold water
4	teaspoons cornstarch

1. In a 5- to 6-quart slow cooker combine potatoes, sweet pepper, and onion. Add chicken.

2. In a medium bowl combine tomatoes, coriander, paprika, ginger, salt, turmeric, crushed red pepper, cinnamon, and cloves; stir in broth. Pour over mixture in cooker.

3. Cover and cook on low-heat setting for 8 to 10 hours or on high-heat setting for 4 to 5 hours.

4. If using low-heat setting, turn to high-heat setting. In a small bowl combine the water and cornstarch; stir into mixture in cooker. Cover and cook for 15 to 20 minutes more or until slightly thickened and bubbly. **Makes 5 servings.**

PER SERVING: 246 cal., 2 g fat (0 g sat. fat), 53 mg chol., 609 mg sodium, 31 g carb., 5 g fiber, 26 g pro.

cook smart Fresh ginger is known to relieve symptoms related to motion sickness as well as nausea and vomiting in pregnancy. Be sure to use a very sharp shredder, such as a Microplane, to grate the ginger because it's so fibrous. Or peel the ginger and very finely chop instead of grating it.

● LOW CALORIE ● GLUTEN FREE

Stirring the shrimp in at the last minute ensures that they stay tender and delicately textured. (Overcooked shrimp gets rubbery and tough.)

chicken and shrimp jambalaya

PREP: 20 minutes   **SLOW COOK:** 4½ hours (low) or 2¼ hours (high) + 30 minutes (high)

1   pound skinless, boneless chicken breast halves or thighs, cut into ¾-inch pieces
2   cups thinly sliced celery (4 stalks)
2   cups chopped onions (2 large)
1   14½-ounce can no-salt-added diced tomatoes, undrained
1   14½-ounce can reduced-sodium chicken broth
½   6-ounce can no-salt-added tomato paste (⅓ cup)
1   recipe Homemade Salt-Free Cajun Seasoning or 1½ teaspoons salt-free Cajun seasoning
2   cloves garlic, minced
½   teaspoon salt
1½ cups uncooked instant brown rice
¾   cup chopped green, red, and/or yellow sweet pepper (1 medium)
8   ounces fresh or frozen peeled and deveined cooked shrimp (tails on if desired)
2   tablespoons snipped fresh Italian (flat-leaf) parsley
Celery leaves (optional)

1. In a 3½- or 4-quart slow cooker combine chicken, celery, onions, tomatoes, broth, tomato paste, Homemade Salt-Free Cajun Seasoning, garlic, and salt.

2. Cover and cook on low-heat setting for 4½ to 5½ hours or on high-heat setting for 2¼ to 2¾ hours.

3. If using low-heat setting, turn cooker to high-heat setting. Stir in uncooked rice and sweet pepper. Cover and cook about 30 minutes more or until most of the liquid is absorbed and rice is tender.

4. To serve, thaw shrimp if frozen. Stir shrimp and parsley into chicken mixture. If desired, garnish each serving with celery leaves. **Makes 8 servings.**

Homemade Salt-Free Cajun Seasoning: In a small bowl stir together ¼ teaspoon ground white pepper, ¼ teaspoon garlic powder, ¼ teaspoon onion powder, ¼ teaspoon paprika, ¼ teaspoon ground black pepper, and ⅛ to ¼ teaspoon cayenne pepper.

PER SERVING: 211 cal., 2 g fat (0 g sat. fat), 88 mg chol., 415 mg sodium, 26 g carb., 4 g fiber, 23 g pro.

If you have leftover burritos, pack one for tomorrow's brown bag lunch. Wrap it in plastic wrap, then in foil. Simply remove the wrappings and reheat it in the microwave when you're ready to eat.

chicken and veggie burritos

PREP: 25 minutes **STAND:** 5 minutes **SLOW COOK:** 6 hours (low) or 2½ hours (high) + 30 minutes

1 large green sweet pepper, cubed
1 cup coarsely chopped onion (1 large)
1 cup coarsely chopped celery (2 stalks)
1½ pounds skinless, boneless chicken breast halves, cut into ½-inch-wide strips
1 8-ounce bottle green taco sauce
1 teaspoon instant chicken bouillon granules
½ teaspoon ground cumin
2 medium zucchini, cut in half lengthwise
½ cup uncooked instant rice
8 9- to 10-inch spinach, chile, or plain flour tortillas, warmed (see tip, page 70)
1 cup chopped tomatoes (2 medium)
¾ cup shredded Monterey Jack cheese with jalapeño peppers (3 ounces)
¼ cup sliced green onions (2)

1. In a 3½- or 4-quart slow cooker combine sweet pepper, onion, and celery. Top with chicken. In a small bowl combine taco sauce, bouillon granules, and cumin. Pour over chicken.

2. Cover and cook on low-heat setting for 6 to 7 hours or on high-heat setting for 2½ to 3 hours. Cut zucchini into ½-inch slices. Stir into mixture in cooker. Cover and cook for 30 minutes more. Stir in rice. Cover and let stand for 5 minutes.

3. To serve, divide chicken mixture evenly among warmed tortillas. Top with tomatoes, cheese, and green onions. Fold bottom edge of each tortilla up and over filling; fold in opposite sides just until they meet. Roll up from the bottom. If necessary, secure with toothpicks. **Makes 8 servings.**

PER SERVING: 328 cal., 8 g fat (3 g sat. fat), 59 mg chol., 603 mg sodium, 35 g carb., 3 g fiber, 27 g pro.

Toasted sesame oil is a potent flavor enhancer. Just 1 tablespoon infuses this Japanese-style dish with warm, nutty flavor.

teriyaki chicken

PREP: 20 minutes   **SLOW COOK:** 5 hours (low) or 2½ hours (high)   **STAND:** 5 minutes

3	to 3½ pounds meaty chicken pieces (breast halves, thighs, and drumsticks), skinned
¼	cup reduced-sodium soy sauce
¼	cup dry sherry
¼	cup water
1	tablespoon toasted sesame oil
1	tablespoon grated fresh ginger
1	tablespoon rice vinegar
2	cloves garlic, minced
6	cups sliced bok choy or shredded Chinese cabbage
2	teaspoons toasted sesame seeds

1. Place chicken in a 3½- or 4-quart slow cooker. In a small bowl stir together soy sauce, sherry, the water, sesame oil, ginger, vinegar, and garlic. Pour over chicken.

2. Cover and cook on low-heat setting for 5 to 6 hours or on high-heat setting for 2½ to 3 hours. Transfer chicken to a serving platter, reserving cooking liquid in cooker. Cover chicken with foil and keep warm.

3. Stir bok choy into liquid in cooker. Cover and let stand for 5 minutes. Transfer bok choy to serving platter with chicken. Sprinkle chicken and bok choy with sesame seeds. If desired, spoon a little of the cooking liquid over chicken and bok choy. **Makes 6 servings.**

PER SERVING: 253 cal., 10 g fat (2 g sat. fat), 92 mg chol., 513 mg sodium, 4 g carb., 1 g fiber, 32 g pro.

For the best flavor, use a white wine in this dish that you would enjoy drinking. There isn't a lot of wine in this recipe, but it does add some flavor. Chardonnay, Sauvignon Blanc, and Pinot Grigio will all work well.

chicken and portobellos with mustard cream

PREP: 15 minutes   **SLOW COOK:** 5 hours (low) or 2½ hours (high)

3	fresh portobello mushroom caps, sliced
2	cloves garlic, minced
3½	to 4 pounds meaty chicken pieces (breast halves, thighs, and drumsticks), skinned
2	teaspoons dried rosemary, crushed
½	teaspoon salt
¼	teaspoon ground black pepper
¼	cup reduced-sodium chicken broth
¼	cup dry white wine
2	cups shredded romaine lettuce
½	cup light sour cream
1	tablespoon country Dijon mustard
	Fresh rosemary sprigs (optional)

1. In a 4- to 5-quart slow cooker combine mushrooms and garlic. Sprinkle chicken with dried rosemary, salt, and pepper. Place chicken in cooker. Pour broth and wine over chicken.

2. Cover and cook on low-heat setting for 5 to 6 hours or on high-heat setting for 2½ to 3 hours.

3. Transfer chicken to a cutting board. Using two forks, pull chicken apart into shreds, discarding bones. Line a serving platter with lettuce; top with shredded chicken. Using a slotted spoon, remove mushrooms from cooker and place on top of chicken. Discard cooking liquid.

4. For mustard cream, in a small bowl combine sour cream and mustard. Serve chicken and mushrooms with mustard cream. If desired, garnish with fresh rosemary. **Makes 6 servings.**

PER SERVING: 209 cal., 7 g fat (2 g sat. fat), 96 mg chol., 393 mg sodium, 4 g carb., 1 g fiber, 31 g pro.

Somen are thin Japanese rice noodles that look like angel hair pasta. They can usually be found in the ethnic section of your local supermarket.

soy-ginger soup with chicken

PREP: 20 minutes   **SLOW COOK:** 4 hours (low) or 2 hours (high) + 3 minutes

1 pound skinless, boneless chicken thighs, cut into 1-inch pieces
1 cup coarsely shredded carrots (2 medium)
2 tablespoons dry sherry (optional)
1 tablespoon soy sauce
1 tablespoon rice vinegar
1 tablespoon grated fresh ginger or ½ tablespoon ground ginger
¼ teaspoon ground black pepper
3 14½-ounce cans reduced-sodium chicken broth
1 cup water
2 ounces dried somen (thin white noodles)
1 6-ounce package frozen snow pea pods, thawed
Soy sauce

1. In a large skillet brown the chicken for 2 to 3 minutes on each side over medium to high heat. Then in a 3½- to 6-quart slow cooker combine chicken, carrots, sherry (if desired), 1 tablespoon soy sauce, vinegar, ginger, and pepper. Stir in broth and the water.

2. Cover and cook on low-heat setting for 4 to 6 hours or on high-heat setting for 2 to 3 hours. Stir in uncooked noodles and frozen pea pods. Cover and cook for 3 minutes more.

3. To serve, ladle soup into bowls and serve with additional soy sauce. **Makes 6 servings.**

PER SERVING: 175 cal., 5 g fat (1 g sat. fat), 72 mg chol., 1,246 mg sodium, 12 g carb., 2 g fiber, 19 g pro.

"Cacciatore" means "hunter" in Italian. Food prepared "hunter-style" features mushrooms, onions, tomatoes, and wine. Chicken prepared hunter-style is the most popular of this type of dish.

cacciatore-style chicken

PREP: 25 minutes   **SLOW COOK:** 6 hours (low) or 3 hours (high) + 15 minutes (high)

2   cups sliced fresh mushrooms
1   cup chopped celery (2 stalks)
1   cup chopped carrots (2 medium)
2   medium onions, cut into wedges
1   yellow, green, or red sweet pepper, cut into thin bite-size strips
4   cloves garlic, minced
12 chicken drumsticks, skinned (about 3½ pounds total)
½   cup chicken broth
¼   cup dry white wine
2   tablespoons quick-cooking tapioca
2   bay leaves
1   teaspoon sugar
1   teaspoon dried oregano, crushed
½   teaspoon salt
¼   teaspoon ground black pepper
1   14½-ounce can diced tomatoes, undrained
⅓   cup tomato paste
    Hot cooked pasta or rice
    Shredded basil (optional)

1. In a 5- to 6-quart slow cooker combine mushrooms, celery, carrots, onions, sweet pepper, and garlic. Place chicken drumsticks on vegetables. In a bowl combine broth, wine, tapioca, bay leaves, sugar, oregano, salt, and black pepper. Pour over mixture in cooker.

2. Cover and cook on low-heat setting for 6 to 7 hours or on high-heat setting for 3 to 3½ hours.

3. Transfer chicken to a serving platter. Cover and keep warm. Discard bay leaves. If using low-heat setting, turn to high-heat setting. Stir in tomatoes and tomato paste. Cover and cook for 15 minutes more.

4. Spoon vegetable mixture over chicken. Serve with hot cooked pasta. If desired, garnish with basil. **Makes 6 servings.**

PER SERVING: 345 cal., 7 g fat (2 g sat. fat), 81 mg chol., 606 mg sodium, 37 g carb., 4 g fiber, 32 g pro.

cook smart Not all whole grain or whole wheat pasta is created equally. To be called whole grain or whole wheat, a whole grain (such as wheat) has to be the ingredient with the highest amount in the product. This means a whole grain product containing 51% of the flour as a whole grain flour and 49% of the flour as white flour can still be considered a whole grain. To get the most whole grain bang for your nutrition buck, look for pasta that uses only whole grain or whole wheat flour.

This five-ingredient recipe (not counting salt and pepper) is aptly named. It goes together in a flash, then slow cooks all day for a satisfying supper that night.

in-a-hurry chicken curry

PREP: 15 minutes   **SLOW COOK:** 6 hours (low) or 3 hours (high)

1   **16-ounce package frozen stew vegetables**
4   **large bone-in chicken thighs (1½ to 1¾ pounds total), skinned**
    Salt
    Ground black pepper
1   **10¾-ounce can condensed cream of potato soup**
2   **teaspoons curry powder**
1   **tablespoon snipped fresh cilantro**

1. Place frozen vegetables in a 3½- or 4-quart slow cooker. Top with chicken. Sprinkle with salt and pepper. In a small bowl stir together soup and curry powder; pour over chicken.

2. Cover and cook on low-heat setting for 6 to 7 hours or on high-heat setting for 3 to 3½ hours.

3. Remove chicken from cooker. Cut chicken off bones; discard bones. If desired, break chicken into large pieces. Return chicken to cooker; stir to combine. Sprinkle each serving with cilantro. **Makes 6 servings.**

PER SERVING: 200 cal., 5 g fat (2 g sat. fat), 97 mg chol., 734 mg sodium, 13 g carb., 1 g fiber, 24 g pro.

You can enjoy this fuss-free French classic any night of the week. It goes well with white or red wine, depending on your mood.

so-easy coq au vin

PREP: 35 minutes   **COOK:** 5 hours (low) or 2½ hours (high)

1	8-ounce package mushrooms, halved (or quartered if large)
4	medium carrots cut into ¼-inch slices
1½	cups frozen pearl onions Nonstick cooking spray
5	to 6 large chicken thighs, skin removed (2¼ to 2½ pounds)
½	teaspoon salt
½	teaspoon ground black pepper
1	cup dry red wine
½	cup reduced-sodium chicken broth
2	tablespoons tapioca
2	tablespoons red wine vinegar
1½	teaspoons herbes de Provence
3	cloves garlic, minced
2	tablespoons snipped fresh Italian (flat-leaf) parsley
4	cups hot cooked whole grain wide noodles

1. In a 4- to 5-quart slow cooker combine mushrooms, carrots, and onions. Set aside.

2. Lightly coat a large nonstick skillet with cooking spray; heat over medium-high heat. Sprinkle both sides of chicken thighs with ¼ teaspoon of the salt and ¼ teaspoon of the pepper. Add chicken thighs to skillet, meaty sides down. Cook about 6 minutes or until brown, turning once. Add chicken to cooker.

3. Add wine to skillet; bring to boiling. Reduce heat; simmer for 2 minutes, using a wooden spoon to scrape up brown bits from bottom and sides of skillet. Remove from heat. Stir in broth, tapioca, vinegar, herbes de Provence, garlic, and the remaining ¼ teaspoon salt and the remaining ¼ teaspoon pepper. Pour over chicken.

4. Cover and cook on low-heat setting for 5 to 5½ hours or on high-heat setting for 2½ to 2¾ hours.

5. Sprinkle with parsley; serve with noodles. **Makes 6 servings.**

PER SERVING: 326 cal., 5 g fat (1 g sat. fat), 80 mg chol., 365 mg sodium, 40 g carb., 6 g fiber, 26 g pro.

● LOW CALORIE

The "stuffing" in this comfort-food classic is actually lightly packed on top of the chicken as it cooks.

chicken with sourdough stuffing

PREP: 20 minutes   **SLOW COOK:** 6 hours (low) or 3 hours (high)

6   cups 1-inch cubes crusty country sourdough bread

1⅓   cups chopped tomatoes (3 medium)

1   cup finely chopped carrots (2 medium)

1½   teaspoons dried thyme, crushed

¼   teaspoon coarse-ground black pepper

½   cup reduced-sodium chicken broth

6   small whole chicken legs (drumstick and thigh), skinned

⅓   cup thinly sliced leek (1 medium) or chopped onion (1 small)

1. For stuffing, in a large bowl combine bread cubes, tomatoes, carrots, thyme, and pepper. Drizzle with broth, tossing gently to moisten. (Stuffing will not be completely moistened.)

2. Place chicken in a 4- to 5-quart slow cooker. Sprinkle with leek. Lightly pack stuffing on top of chicken.

3. Cover and cook on low-heat setting for 6 to 6½ hours or on high-heat setting for 3 to 3½ hours. **Makes 6 servings.**

PER SERVING: 270 cal., 6 g fat (1 g sat. fat), 104 mg chol., 379 mg sodium, 22 g carb., 2 g fiber, 30 g pro.

cook smart Leeks can be used in place of onions in many recipes to add different flavor. Leeks need to be cleaned well, and you should only use the white and very light green part of the stalk. Trim a thin slice off the base and cut off the top where the green part starts to darken. Split the remaining portion in half lengthwise and open the leek to expose the layers. Rinse the layers well in cold water. Thinly slice the leek crosswise or chop to use.

Slow cooking gives the chicken ample time to absorb the sweet and spicy flavors of the thick, dark sauce.

simple hoisin chicken

PREP: 15 minutes   **SLOW COOK:** 4 hours (low) or 2½ hours (high) + 30 minutes (high)

	Nonstick cooking spray
12	bone-in chicken thighs (3½ to 4 pounds total), skinned
2	tablespoons quick-cooking tapioca
⅛	teaspoon salt
⅛	teaspoon ground black pepper
½	cup hoisin sauce
1	16-ounce package frozen broccoli stir-fry vegetables
3	cups hot cooked rice

1. Coat the inside of a 3½- or 4-quart slow cooker with cooking spray. Place chicken in the prepared cooker. Sprinkle chicken with tapioca, salt, and pepper. Pour hoisin sauce over chicken.

2. Cover and cook on low-heat setting for 4 to 5 hours or on high-heat setting for 2½ hours.

3. If using low-heat setting, turn to high-heat setting. Stir in frozen vegetables. Cover and cook for 30 to 45 minutes more or just until vegetables are tender. Serve over hot cooked rice. **Makes 6 servings.**

PER SERVING: 345 cal., 6 g fat (2 g sat. fat), 115 mg chol., 537 mg sodium, 37 g carb., 3 g fiber, 32 g pro.

● LOW CALORIE   ● GLUTEN FREE

Serve this Indian-style stew with warm wedges of naan, a traditional Indian flatbread that is increasingly available in grocery stores and the food sections of big-box stores.

garam masala chicken stew with peas and potatoes

PREP: 20 minutes   **SLOW COOK:** 5¼ hours (low) or 2¾ hours (high) + 15 minutes (high)

	Nonstick cooking spray
6	large skinless, boneless chicken thighs (about 1½ pounds)
12	ounces red potatoes, cut into ½-inch cubes (4 small or 2 medium)
1	medium onion, thinly sliced
1½	teaspoons grated fresh ginger
2	cloves garlic, minced
½	teaspoon salt
½	teaspoon ground black pepper
1	14½-ounce can reduced-sodium chicken broth
1	8-ounce can no-salt-added tomato sauce
1	cup frozen peas
½	cup plain fat-free yogurt
2	teaspoons garam masala

1. Lightly coat a large skillet with cooking spray. Heat skillet over medium-high heat. Add chicken thighs, meaty sides down; cook about 6 minutes or until brown on both sides, turning once.

2. In a 3½- or 4-quart slow cooker combine potatoes, onion, ginger, and garlic. Top with chicken. Sprinkle with salt and pepper. Pour broth and tomato sauce over all.

3. Cover and cook on low-heat setting for 5½ hours or on high-heat setting for 2¾ hours.

4. If using low-heat setting, turn to high-heat setting. Stir in peas, yogurt, and garam masala. Cover and cook for 15 minutes more. **Makes 6 servings.**

PER SERVING: 239 cal., 5 g fat (1 g sat. fat), 95 mg chol., 510 mg sodium, 20 g carb., 4 g fiber, 28 g pro.

When cutting up the fennel, use the white bulb—not the stalks or feathery green fronds. Save the stalks for a batch of homemade stock. The fronds make a nice garnish in place of the parsley if you like.

braised chicken with fennel and cannellini

PREP: 25 minutes   **SLOW COOK:** 5 hours (low) or 2½ hours (high)

2	to 2½ pounds chicken drumsticks and/or thighs, skinned
¾	teaspoon salt
¼	teaspoon ground black pepper
1	15-ounce can cannellini (white kidney) beans, rinsed and drained
1	medium fennel bulb, cored and cut into thin wedges
1	medium yellow sweet pepper, seeded and cut into 1-inch pieces
1	medium onion, cut into thin wedges
3	cloves garlic, minced
1	teaspoon snipped fresh rosemary
1	teaspoon snipped fresh oregano
¼	teaspoon crushed red pepper
1	14½-ounce can diced tomatoes, undrained
½	cup dry white wine or reduced-sodium chicken broth
¼	cup tomato paste
¼	cup shaved Parmesan cheese (1 ounce)
1	tablespoon snipped fresh Italian (flat-leaf) parsley

1. Sprinkle chicken with ¼ teaspoon of the salt and the black pepper. Place chicken in a 3½- or 4-quart slow cooker. Top with drained beans, fennel, sweet pepper, onion, garlic, rosemary, oregano, and crushed red pepper. In a medium bowl combine tomatoes, wine, tomato paste, and the remaining ½ teaspoon salt; pour over mixture in cooker.

2. Cover and cook on low-heat setting for 5 to 6 hours or on high-heat setting for 2½ to 3 hours.

3. Sprinkle each serving with cheese and parsley. **Makes 6 servings.**

PER SERVING: 225 cal., 4 g fat (1 g sat. fat), 68 mg chol., 777 mg sodium, 23 g carb., 7 g fiber, 25 g pro.

cook smart Fennel is a crunchy vegetable that tastes a bit like anise. To use a fennel bulb, cut off the upper stalks and trim a thin slice from the base of the bulb. Cut the bulb into thin wedges and remove the core from the center.

Chicken and hearty vegetables simmer in a delicate wine-flavor sauce. Choose dark-meat chicken—legs, thighs, or drumsticks—for this dish.

chicken with wine sauce

PREP: 30 minutes   **SLOW COOK:** 7 hours (low) or 3½ hours (high)

4	medium round red potatoes, quartered
4	medium carrots, cut into ½-inch pieces
2	stalks celery, cut into 1-inch pieces
1	small onion, sliced
3	pounds bone-in chicken thighs or drumsticks, skinned
1	tablespoon snipped fresh Italian (flat-leaf) parsley
1	clove garlic, minced
½	teaspoon salt
½	teaspoon dried rosemary, crushed
½	teaspoon dried thyme, crushed
¼	teaspoon ground black pepper
1	cup reduced-sodium chicken broth
½	cup dry white wine
3	tablespoons butter
3	tablespoons all-purpose flour
	Snipped fresh thyme (optional)

1. In a 5- to 6-quart slow cooker combine potatoes, carrots, celery, and onion. Place chicken on top of vegetables. Sprinkle with parsley, garlic, salt, rosemary, thyme, and pepper. Pour broth and wine over mixture in cooker.

2. Cover and cook on low-heat setting for 7 to 8 hours or on high-heat setting for 3½ to 4 hours.

3. Using a slotted spoon, transfer chicken and vegetables to a serving platter. Cover with foil and keep warm.

4. For sauce, skim fat from cooking liquid; strain liquid. In a large saucepan heat butter over medium heat until melted. Stir in flour; cook for 1 minute. Add cooking liquid. Cook and stir until thickened and bubbly. Cook and stir for 1 minute more.

5. If desired, sprinkle chicken and vegetables with fresh thyme. Serve with sauce. **Makes 6 servings.**

PER SERVING: 321 cal., 11 g fat (5 g sat. fat), 122 mg chol., 463 mg sodium, 23 g carb., 3 g fiber, 29 g pro.

The whole family will love the melty goodness of these satisfying open-face sandwiches.

italian-herbed chicken and mozzarella melts

PREP: 20 minutes **SLOW COOK:** 6½ hours (low) or 3¼ hours (high) **BROIL:** 2 minutes

Nonstick cooking spray

8 skinless, boneless chicken thighs (about 2 pounds total)

2 medium green sweet peppers, thinly sliced

½ teaspoon dried rosemary, crushed

1 cup bottled spaghetti sauce

½ cup coarsely chopped pitted Kalamata olives

1 cup shredded part-skim mozzarella cheese (4 ounces)

¼ cup snipped fresh basil

2 tablespoons grated Parmesan cheese

8 slices whole grain Italian bread

1. Lightly coat a 3½- or 4-quart slow cooker with cooking spray. Lightly coat a large nonstick skillet with cooking spray. Heat the skillet over medium-high heat. Add chicken; cook about 2 minutes or until light brown on both sides, turning once.

2. Place sweet peppers in prepared cooker. Top with chicken. Sprinkle with rosemary. Pour spaghetti sauce over chicken.

3. Cover and cook on low-heat setting for 6½ to 7 hours or on high-heat setting for 3¼ to 3½ hours.

4. Preheat broiler. Line a baking sheet with foil; set aside. Using a slotted spoon, transfer peppers and chicken to a medium bowl, reserving cooking juices. Using two forks, pull chicken apart into coarse shreds. Add olives to chicken. In a small bowl combine mozzarella cheese, basil, and Parmesan cheese.

5. Place bread on prepared baking sheet. Broil 4 to 5 inches from the heat for 1 to 2 minutes or until toasted. Turn over bread slices. Top each slice with some of the chicken mixture; drizzle each with about 1 tablespoon of the cooking juices. Sprinkle each with cheese mixture. Broil 1 to 2 minutes more or until toasted and cheese is melted. **Makes 8 servings.**

PER SERVING: 296 cal., 10 g fat (3 g sat. fat), 104 mg chol., 561 mg sodium, 20 g carb., 6 g fiber, 32 g pro.

Even though this dish uses frozen artichokes, it's nice and light for spring, when fresh artichokes are in season.

garlic chicken with artichokes

PREP: 20 minutes   **SLOW COOK:** 5 hours (low) or 2½ hours (high) + 30 minutes (high)

2   medium red sweet peppers, cut into 1-inch-wide strips

2   medium onions, cut into wedges

12   cloves garlic, peeled

1   tablespoon quick-cooking tapioca

2   teaspoons dried rosemary, crushed

1   teaspoon finely shredded lemon peel

½   teaspoon ground black pepper

½   cup chicken broth

3   pounds skinless, boneless chicken thighs

1   8- to 9-ounce package frozen artichoke hearts

1   tablespoon lemon juice

4   cups hot cooked brown rice

1. In a 3½- or 4-quart slow cooker combine sweet peppers, onions, garlic, tapioca, rosemary, lemon peel, and black pepper. Pour broth over mixture in cooker. Add chicken.

2. Cover and cook on low-heat setting for 5 hours or on high-heat setting for 2½ hours. If using low-heat setting, turn cooker to high-heat setting. Stir in frozen artichoke hearts and lemon juice. Cover and cook 30 to 60 minutes more. Serve with rice. **Makes 8 servings.**

PER SERVING: 358 cal., 8 g fat (2 g sat. fat), 141 mg chol., 233 mg sodium, 32 g carb., 5 g fiber, 38 g pro.

● LOW CALORIE ● GLUTEN FREE

Depending on what you like and have on hand, this recipe works well with both red curry powder or paste (which has traditional curry ingredients plus chile powder) and yellow curry powder or paste.

coconut-chicken curry stew

PREP: 20 minutes **SLOW COOK:** 6 hours (low) or 3 hours (high)

Nonstick cooking spray
1 **pound skinless, boneless chicken thighs, cut into 1-inch pieces**
3 **cups chopped carrots (6 medium)**
2 **cups coarsely chopped onions (2 large)**
6 **cloves garlic, minced**
1 **tablespoon grated fresh ginger**
1 **14½-ounce can reduced-sodium chicken broth**
1 **cup light coconut milk**
1 **tablespoon curry powder**
½ **teaspoon salt**
¼ **cup snipped fresh cilantro**
1 **tablespoon lemon juice**

1. Coat a medium nonstick skillet with cooking spray. Heat over medium-high heat; add chicken. Cook and stir about 3 minutes or until light brown. Drain off fat

2. In a 3½- or 4-quart slow cooker layer carrots, chicken, onions, garlic, and ginger.

3. In a medium bowl whisk together broth, coconut milk, curry powder, and salt. Pour over the mixture in cooker.

4. Cover and cook on low-heat setting for 6 to 8 hours or on high-heat setting for 3 to 4 hours.

5. To serve, stir in cilantro and lemon juice. **Makes 6 servings.**

PER SERVING: 174 cal., 5 g fat (2 g sat. fat), 63 mg chol., 478 mg sodium, 15 g carb., 3 g fiber, 17 g pro.

Here's the secret to gorgeous, unbruised avocados: Buy them when they are unripe, with light green skin, and ripen them at home for 2 to 3 days. When they are very firm, they don't bruise in transit.

spicy chipotle chicken lentil stew

PREP: 20 minutes   **SLOW COOK:** 10 hours (low) or 5 hours (high)

2   cups sliced carrots (4 medium)
8   ounces skinless, boneless chicken breast halves, cut into 1-inch pieces
8   ounces skinless, boneless chicken thighs, cut into 1-inch pieces
1   cup brown lentils, rinsed
1   cup chopped onion (1 large)
1   tablespoon finely chopped canned chipotle peppers in adobo sauce (see tip, page 14)
1   tablespoon chili powder
2   teaspoons ground cumin
1½ teaspoons dried oregano, crushed
2   cloves garlic, minced
3   14½-ounce cans reduced-sodium chicken broth
1   14½-ounce can Italian-style stewed tomatoes, undrained and cut up
1   10-ounce can diced tomatoes and green chiles, undrained
½   cup shredded Monterey jack cheese (2 ounces)
    Avocado slices (optional)
    Plain fat-free yogurt (optional)

1. In a 5- to 6-quart slow cooker layer carrots, chicken, lentils, onion, chipotle peppers, chili powder, cumin, oregano, and garlic. Add broth, stewed tomatoes, and tomatoes and green chiles.

2. Cover and cook on low-heat setting for 10 hours or on high-heat setting for 5 hours.

3. Serve topped with cheese and, if desired, avocado slices and yogurt. **Makes 8 servings.**

PER SERVING: 236 cal., 4 g fat (2 g sat. fat), 46 mg chol., 737 mg sodium, 26 g carb., 10 g fiber, 24 g pro.

The peanut butter stirred into this soup gives it a pleasantly nutty flavor.

red bean, chicken, and sweet potato stew

PREP: 20 minutes   **SLOW COOK:** 10 hours (low) or 5 hours (high)

2   **15-ounce cans no-salt-added red beans, rinsed and drained**
4   **cups peeled, cubed sweet potatoes (about 1 pound)**
8   **ounces boneless chicken breasts, cut into bite-size pieces**
8   **ounces boneless chicken thighs, cut into bite-size pieces**
2   **14½-ounce cans reduced-sodium chicken broth**
2½ **cups chopped green sweet peppers (2 large)**
1   **14½-ounce can no-salt-added diced tomatoes, undrained**
1   **10-ounce can tomatoes and chopped green chiles, undrained**
1   **tablespoon Cajun seasoning**
2   **cloves garlic, minced**
¼   **cup creamy peanut butter**
    Snipped fresh cilantro
    Chopped peanuts (optional)

1. In a 5- to 6-quart slow cooker combine beans, sweet potatoes, chicken, broth, sweet peppers, diced tomatoes, tomatoes and green chiles, Cajun seasoning, and garlic.

2. Cover and cook on low-heat setting for 10 to 12 hours or on high-heat setting for 5 to 6 hours.

3. Remove 1 cup hot liquid from cooker. Whisk in peanut butter. Stir into mixture in cooker.

4. Serve topped with cilantro and, if desired, peanuts. **Makes 6 servings.**

PER SERVING: 366 cal., 7 g fat (2 g sat. fat), 53 mg chol., 830 mg sodium, 46 g carb., 16 g fiber, 32 g pro.

It's not easy being green—unless you're referring to this veggie-rich chicken chowder packed with edamame, green sweet pepper, and zucchini.

chicken-edamame chowder

PREP: 30 minutes **SLOW COOK:** 7 hours (low) or 3½ hours (low) + 20 minutes (high)

1 tablespoon vegetable oil

1 pound skinless, boneless chicken breast halves, cut into 1-inch pieces

1 12-ounce package frozen sweet soybeans (edamame)

1¼ cups coarsely chopped green sweet pepper (1 large)

1 cup chopped onion (1 large)

2 fresh jalapeño peppers, seeded and finely chopped (see tip, page 14)

2 teaspoons ground cumin

2 teaspoons ground coriander

½ teaspoon salt

¼ teaspoon ground black pepper

2 14½-ounce cans chicken broth

1 8-ounce carton sour cream

3 tablespoons all-purpose flour

2 medium zucchini, halved lengthwise

Shredded Monterey Jack cheese (optional)

Snipped fresh cilantro (optional)

1. In a large skillet heat oil over medium-high heat. Add chicken; cook and stir until light brown. In a 3½- or 4-quart slow cooker combine chicken, frozen soybeans, sweet pepper, onion, jalapeño peppers, cumin, coriander, salt, and black pepper. Pour broth over mixture in cooker. Stir to combine.

2. Cover and cook on low-heat setting for 7 to 8 hours or on high-heat setting for 3½ to 4 hours.

3. If using low-heat setting, turn to high-heat setting. In a small bowl combine sour cream and flour. Thinly slice zucchini. Stir sour cream mixture and zucchini into chicken mixture. Cover and cook for 20 to 30 minutes more or until mixture is thickened and zucchini is crisp-tender.

4. If desired, serve topped with cheese and cilantro. **Makes 6 servings.**

PER SERVING: 314 cal., 14 g fat (6 g sat. fat), 62 mg chol., 806 mg sodium, 17 g carb., 8 g fiber, 28 g pro.

● **LOW CALORIE**

Some folks say homemade chicken noodle soup helps battle a cold or flu, but even doubters agree its comforting flavor has great appeal. This rich and creamy version serves a crowd.

creamy chicken noodle soup

PREP: 25 minutes   **SLOW COOK:** 6 hours (low) or 3 hours (high) + 20 minutes (high)

1	32-ounce container reduced-sodium chicken broth
3	cups water
2½	cups chopped cooked chicken (about 12 ounces)
1½	cups sliced carrots (3 medium)
1½	cups sliced celery (3 stalks)
1½	cups mushrooms, sliced (4 ounces)
¼	cup chopped onion
1½	teaspoons dried thyme, crushed
¾	teaspoon garlic pepper
3	ounces reduced-fat cream cheese (Neufchâtel), cut up
2	cups dried egg noodles

1. In a 5- to 6-quart slow cooker combine chicken broth, the water, chicken, carrots, celery, mushrooms, onion, thyme, and garlic pepper.

2. Cover and cook on low-heat setting for 6 to 8 hours or on high-heat setting for 3 to 4 hours.

3. If using low-heat setting, turn to high-heat setting. Stir in cream cheese until combined. Stir in uncooked noodles. Cover and cook for 20 to 30 minutes more or just until noodles are tender. **Makes 8 servings.**

PER SERVING: 170 cal., 6 g fat (2 g sat. fat), 54 mg chol., 401 mg sodium, 11 g carb., 2 g fiber, 17 g pro.

Quinoa substitutes easily for rice in main dishes, side dishes, soups, and salads—even puddings. Quinoa is high in protein, fiber, and vitamin A and is lower in carbohydrate than most grains.

quinoa with sausage and peppers

PREP: 25 minutes   **SLOW COOK:** 4 hours (low) or 2 hours (high)

1   14½-ounce can reduced-sodium chicken broth
1   cup quinoa, rinsed and drained
¼   cup cider vinegar
2   tablespoons stone-ground mustard
2   teaspoons honey
3   medium yellow, green, and/or red sweet peppers, cut into bite-size pieces
1   medium sweet onion, cut into thin wedges
2   12-ounce packages cooked Italian chicken sausage links, halved lengthwise and sliced crosswise
1   cup shredded reduced-fat cheddar cheese or crumbled reduced-fat feta cheese (4 ounces)

1. In a 4- to 5-quart slow cooker combine broth, quinoa, vinegar, mustard, and honey. Add sweet peppers, onion, and sausage.

2. Cover and cook on low-heat setting for 4 to 5 hours or on high-heat setting for 2 to 2½ hours.

3. To serve, stir mixture gently. Top each serving with cheese. **Makes 8 servings.**

PER SERVING: 279 cal., 11 g fat (4 g sat. fat), 74 mg chol., 772 mg sodium, 22 g carb., 2 g fiber, 23 g pro.

● HIGH FIBER   ● GLUTEN FREE

Last-minute additions of oranges and sliced green onions add a fresh touch to this island-style dish.

jamaican jerk chicken

PREP: 25 minutes   **SLOW COOK:** 5 hours (low) or 2½ hours (high)

1   20-ounce can pineapple chunks (juice pack)

1¾ pounds skinless, boneless chicken thighs, cut into 1-inch pieces

1   15-ounce can black beans, rinsed and drained

1   small fresh jalapeño pepper, seeded and finely chopped (see tip, page 14)

6   tablespoons finely chopped green onions (3)

2   tablespoons quick-cooking tapioca

2   tablespoons red wine vinegar

1   tablespoon Dijon mustard

4   to 6 teaspoons salt-free jerk seasoning

½   teaspoon salt

¼   teaspoon ground black pepper

1   orange, peeled and sectioned

2   cups hot cooked brown rice
    Sliced green onions (optional)

1. Drain pineapple, reserving juice. In a 3½- or 4-quart slow cooker place chicken, pineapple chunks, beans, jalapeño pepper, and green onions.

2. In a small bowl combine reserved pineapple juice, tapioca, vinegar, mustard, jerk seasoning, salt, and black pepper; pour into cooker.

3. Cover and cook on low-heat setting for 5 to 5½ hours or on high-heat setting for 2½ to 2¾ hours.

4. To serve, stir in orange sections. Serve with hot cooked rice and, if desired, sliced green onions. **Makes 6 servings.**

PER SERVING: 378 cal., 6 g fat (1 g sat. fat), 110 mg chol., 621 mg sodium, 50 g carb., 7 g fiber, 35 g pro.

Who needs a grill to barbecue? These saucy thighs hold their form nicely during slow-heat cooking and hold their own against grilled turkey dishes any day.

spiced barbecue turkey thighs

PREP: 20 minutes   **SLOW COOK:** 9 hours (low) or 4½ hours (high)

½ cup ketchup
2 tablespoons sugar
1 tablespoon quick-cooking tapioca
1 tablespoon cider vinegar
1 teaspoon Worcestershire sauce
¼ teaspoon ground cinnamon
¼ teaspoon crushed red pepper
2 to 2½ pounds turkey thighs or meaty chicken pieces (breast halves, thighs, and drumsticks), skinned
2 cups hot cooked brown rice or whole wheat pasta (optional)
   Fresh cilantro leaves (optional)

1. In a 3½- or 4-quart slow cooker combine ketchup, sugar, tapioca, vinegar, Worcestershire sauce, cinnamon, and crushed red pepper. Place turkey thighs, meaty sides down, on top of mixture in cooker.

2. Cover and cook on low-heat setting for 9 to 10 hours or on high-heat setting for 4½ to 5 hours.

3. Transfer turkey to a cutting board. When turkey is cool enough to handle, remove meat from bones; discard bones. Coarsely chop or shred turkey. Pour cooking juices into a large bowl; skim off fat. Stir turkey into cooking juices.

4. If desired, serve turkey over hot cooked rice. If desired, garnish with cilantro. **Makes 4 servings.**

PER SERVING: 226 cal., 4 g fat (1 g sat. fat), 116 mg chol., 447 mg sodium, 17 g carb., 0 g fiber, 30 g pro.

Spelt is an ancient cereal grain with a nutty, mellow flavor. It's related to wheat, but it's higher in protein and more easily digested. Look for it at health food stores.

tomatillo-turkey chili with spelt

PREP: 15 minutes   **SLOW COOK:** 3½ hours (high)

Nonstick cooking spray
1   pound skinless, boneless turkey breast (or thigh), cut into 1-inch cubes
1   16-ounce jar tomatillo salsa (salsa verde)
1   15- to 15½-ounce can Great Northern or cannellini beans (white kidney beans), rinsed and drained
1   14½-ounce can reduced-sodium chicken broth
1½   cups whole spelt, rinsed
½   cup coarsely chopped onion (1 medium)
1   tablespoon ground cumin
2   cloves garlic, crushed
½   teaspoon ground coriander
¼   teaspoon salt
½   cup chopped red onion (1 small)
1   medium lime, cut into wedges

1. Lightly coat a large skillet with cooking spray. Heat skillet over medium heat. Add turkey; cook and stir until brown on all sides.

2. In a 3½- or 4-quart slow cooker combine turkey, salsa, beans, broth, spelt, ½ cup chopped onion, the cumin, garlic, coriander, and salt.

3. Cover and cook on high-heat setting about 3½ hours or until spelt is tender.

4. Sprinkle each serving with some of the ½ cup red onion. Serve with lime wedges. **Makes 5 servings.**

PER SERVING: 425 cal., 3 g fat (1 g sat. fat), 56 mg chol., 857 mg sodium, 64 g carb., 12 g fiber, 39 g pro.

● LOW CALORIE ● GLUTEN FREE

Top this comforting and creamy low-fat soup with a combination of toasted nuts and dried cranberries for a crunchy surprise.

creamy turkey soup

PREP: 30 minutes **SLOW COOK:** 9 hours (low) or 4½ hours (high) + 45 minutes (high)

8   ounces red-skin potatoes, cut into 1-inch pieces
8   ounces cremini mushrooms, sliced
1   cup coarsely chopped onion (1 large)
1   cup sliced celery (2 stalks)
2   turkey breast tenderloins (about 1½ pounds total)
3   14½-ounce cans reduced-sodium chicken broth
1½ teaspoons dried thyme, crushed
½   teaspoon ground black pepper
1   12-ounce can (1½ cups) evaporated fat-free milk
3   tablespoons cornstarch
½   cup sliced green onions (4)
2   tablespoons lemon juice
    Toasted sliced almonds or chopped pecans (see tip, page 23) and/or dried cranberries (optional)

1. In a 6-quart slow cooker combine potatoes, mushrooms, onion, and celery. Top with turkey. Add broth, thyme, and pepper.

2. Cover and cook on low-heat setting for 9 to 10 hours or on high-heat setting for 4½ to 5 hours.

3. Transfer turkey to a cutting board; use two forks to pull turkey apart into shreds. Return to cooker. In a small bowl stir together evaporated milk and cornstarch; stir into mixture in cooker. If using low-heat setting, turn cooker to high-heat setting.

4. Cover and cook for 45 to 60 minutes more or until bubbly on edges. Stir in green onions and lemon juice.

5. If desired, serve topped with nuts and/or cranberries. **Makes 8 servings.**

PER SERVING: 188 cal., 1 g fat (0 g sat. fat), 39 mg chol., 487 mg sodium, 18 g carb., 2 g fiber, 26 g pro.

Substitute lower-carb or whole grain tortillas for the regular flour tortillas if you like.

sesame-ginger turkey wraps

PREP: 20 minutes   **SLOW COOK:** 6 hours (low) or 3 hours (high)   **STAND:** 5 minutes

Nonstick cooking spray
3   skinless turkey thighs (3½ to 4 pounds)
1   cup bottled sesame-ginger stir-fry sauce
¼   cup water
1   16-ounce package shredded broccoli (broccoli slaw mix)
12   8-inch flour tortillas, warmed (see tip, page 70)
¾   cup sliced green onions (6)

1. Lightly coat a 3½- or 4-quart slow cooker with cooking spray. Place turkey in prepared cooker. In a small bowl stir together stir-fry sauce and the water. Pour over turkey.

2. Cover and cook on low-heat setting for 6 to 7 hours or on high-heat setting for 3 to 3½ hours.

3. Transfer turkey to a cutting board; cool slightly. Remove turkey from bones; discard bones. Using two forks, pull turkey apart into shreds. Return to mixture in cooker. Stir broccoli into mixture in cooker. Cover; let stand for 5 minutes. Using a slotted spoon remove turkey mixture from cooker.

4. To serve, place some of the turkey mixture on each tortilla. Top with green onions. If desired, spoon some of the cooking juices from cooker on top of green onions. Roll up and serve immediately. **Makes 12 servings.**

PER SERVING: 207 cal., 5 g fat (1 g sat. fat), 67 mg chol., 422 mg sodium, 20 g carb., 2 g fiber, 20 g pro.

It only tastes like Friday night! All of your favorite pizza flavors are combined in one nutritious stew that makes an excellent weeknight meal.

pizza stew with biscuits

PREP: 20 minutes   **SLOW COOK:** 3 hours (low) + 45 minutes (high)

8	ounces cremini mushrooms, quartered or sliced
¾	cup chopped green sweet pepper (1 medium)
⅓	cup finely chopped onion (1 small)
1	teaspoon dried Italian seasoning, crushed
¼	teaspoon salt
¼	teaspoon ground black pepper
2	cups marinara sauce
1¼	pounds uncooked ground turkey breast
¾	cup low-fat pancake and baking mix
⅓	cup grated Parmesan cheese
¼	teaspoon dried oregano, crushed
¼	cup fat-free milk
½	cup shredded part-skim mozzarella cheese (2 ounces) (optional)

1. In a 3½- or 4-quart slow cooker combine mushrooms, sweet pepper, onion, Italian seasoning, salt, and black pepper. Pour marinara sauce over all. Using a wooden spoon, break up ground turkey into bite-size pieces. Add to cooker, stirring to combine.

2. Cover and cook on low-heat setting for 3 hours.

3. In a small bowl combine baking mix, Parmesan cheese, and oregano. Add milk; stir with a fork until combined.

4. Turn cooker to high-heat setting. Drop dumpling mixture by tablespoons into five mounds onto mixture in cooker, spacing the mounds evenly.

5. Cover and cook for 45 to 60 minutes more or until a toothpick inserted into the centers of dumplings comes out clean.

6. To serve, if desired, sprinkle each serving with mozzarella cheese. **Makes 5 servings.**

PER SERVING: 323 cal., 7 g fat (2 g sat. fat), 62 mg chol., 851 mg sodium, 32 g carb., 4 g fiber, 33 g pro.

Use your favorite salsa—mild, medium, hot, or even salsa verde—as a tasty topper for this stew.

turkey tortilla stew

PREP: 15 minutes   **SLOW COOK:** 6 hours (low) or 3 hours (high)   **BAKE:** 8 minutes at 400°F

1¼ **pounds turkey breast tenderloin, cut into 1-inch pieces**
1 **14½-ounce can diced tomatoes, undrained**
1 **cup chopped onion (1 large)**
¾ **cup chopped green sweet pepper (1 medium)**
½ **cup reduced-sodium chicken broth**
3 **tablespoons tomato paste**
2 **teaspoons ground cumin**
2 **teaspoons chili powder**
½ **teaspoon ground black pepper**
¼ **teaspoon salt**
4 **6-inch corn tortillas, cut into ¼-inch-thick strips**
   Nonstick cooking spray
⅛ **teaspoon salt**
¼ **cup plain nonfat Greek yogurt**
2 **tablespoons salsa**
1 **avocado, halved, seeded, peeled, and sliced**
2 **fresh limes, cut into wedges**

1. In a 3½- or 4-quart slow cooker combine turkey, tomatoes, onion, sweet pepper, broth, tomato paste, cumin, chili powder, black pepper, and the ¼ teaspoon salt.

2. Cover and cook on low-heat setting for 6 hours or on high-heat setting for 3 hours.

3. Meanwhile, preheat oven to 400°F. Spread tortillas on a large baking sheet; coat with cooking spray. Sprinkle with the ⅛ teaspoon salt; toss and spread into an even layer. Bake for 8 to 12 minutes or until golden, tossing once halfway through baking.

4. To serve, ladle stew into serving bowls. Top each serving with yogurt and salsa. Garnish each serving with tortilla strips, avocado, and a lime wedge. **Makes 4 servings.**

PER SERVING: 353 cal., 7 g fat (1 g sat. fat), 88 mg chol., 746 mg sodium, 33 g carb., 9 g fiber, 41 g pro.

These fork-optional sandwiches are just plain fun. They're perfect for pizza-and-movie night at your house when you'd like a more healthful option than frozen pizza or delivery.

open-face pizza sandwiches

PREP: 25 minutes   **SLOW COOK:** 4 hours (low) or 2 hours (high)

1	teaspoon olive oil
12	ounces uncooked ground Italian turkey sausage
	Nonstick cooking spray
4½	cups sliced mushrooms (12 ounces)
2½	cups chopped green sweet peppers (2 large)
1½	cups chopped onions (3 medium)
1	8-ounce can pizza sauce
½	teaspoon dried oregano, crushed
¼	teaspoon crushed red pepper
4	ciabatta rolls, split and toasted
1	cup shredded part-skim mozzarella (4 ounces)

1. In a nonstick skillet heat oil over medium heat. Add turkey sausage; cook until brown, using a wooden spoon to break up meat as it cooks. Drain off fat.

2. Coat a 3½- or 4-quart slow cooker with cooking spray. In cooker combine sausage, mushrooms, sweet peppers, onions, pizza sauce, oregano, and crushed red pepper.

3. Cover and cook on low-heat setting for 4 to 4½ hours or on high-heat setting for 2 to 2¼ hours.

4. Using a slotted spoon, divide sausage mixture evenly among roll halves. Top each with some of the cheese. **Makes 8 servings.**

PER SERVING: 289 cal., 8 g fat (4 g sat. fat), 35 mg chol., 790 mg sodium, 39 g carb., 4 g fiber, 18 g pro.

Italian-style turkey meatballs get a makeover in this flavorful Mexican stew. Top it with crushed red pepper to add a little heat.

mexican meatball stew

PREP: 10 minutes   **SLOW COOK:** 6 hours (low) or 3 hours (high)

2   14½-ounce cans Mexican-style stewed tomatoes, undrained

2   12-ounce packages frozen cooked Italian-style turkey meatballs, thawed (24 total)

1   15-ounce can black beans, rinsed and drained

1   14½-ounce can seasoned chicken broth with roasted garlic

1   10-ounce package frozen whole kernel corn, thawed
    Fresh oregano (optional)

1. In a 4- to 5-quart slow cooker combine tomatoes, meatballs, beans, broth, and corn.

2. Cover and cook on low-heat setting for 6 to 7 hours or on high-heat setting for 3 to 3½ hours. If desired, garnish each serving with oregano. **Makes 8 servings.**

PER SERVING: 287 cal., 13 g fat (6 g sat. fat), 37 mg chol., 1,134 mg sodium, 30 g carb., 6 g fiber, 16 g pro.

cook smart The ingredients for this quick-to-fix stew can be kept on hand in the pantry and freezer for those days when you need a hot meal and haven't been able to get to the grocery store.

meatless

Slow cookers aren't just for simmering big pieces of meat. They handily cook up whole grains, legumes, pasta sauces, and vegetables.

Creamy cubes of tofu give this one-dish meal an ample dose of protein; veggies give it a healthful spin.

cheesy noodle casserole

PREP: 25 minutes   **SLOW COOK:** 7 hours (low) or 3½ hours (high) + 20 minutes (high)

2½   cups water
1   10¾-ounce can reduced-fat and reduced-sodium condensed cream of mushroom soup
1   14½-ounce can no-salt-added diced tomatoes, undrained
1   cup sliced celery (2 stalks)
1   cup sliced carrots (2 medium)
1   cup chopped onion (1 large)
1½   teaspoons dried Italian seasoning, crushed
2   cloves garlic, minced
¼   teaspoon salt
¼   teaspoon ground black pepper
8   ounces dried extra-wide noodles
1   16-ounce package extra-firm tofu (fresh bean curd), drained, if necessary, and cubed*
½   cup shredded reduced-fat cheddar cheese (2 ounces)

1. In a 3½- or 4-quart slow cooker whisk together the water and cream of mushroom soup. Stir in tomatoes, celery, carrots, onion, Italian seasoning, garlic, salt, and pepper.

2. Cover and cook on low-heat setting for 7 to 8 hours or high-heat setting for 3½ to 4 hours.

3. If using low-heat setting, turn to high-heat setting. Stir in uncooked noodles; cover and cook for 20 to 30 minutes more or until tender, stirring once halfway through cooking. Gently stir in tofu cubes. Sprinkle with cheese; cover and let stand until cheese is melted. **Makes 6 servings.**

*****Tip:** To drain tofu, place it on a paper towel-lined plate for 15 minutes.

PER SERVING: 316 cal., 8 g fat (2 g sat. fat), 44 mg chol., 447 mg sodium, 42 g carb., 4 g fiber, 17 g pro.

cook smart Tofu, made from soybeans, is a hearty substitute for meat and very versatile because it doesn't have a lot of flavor on its own but soaks up a lot of flavor from ingredients with which it's paired. Soy protein from foods like tofu can help prevent heart disease.

Traditional risotto calls for frequent stirring and constant attention. This unwatched-pot version produces creamy, satisfying results.

asparagus and mushroom "risotto"

PREP: 25 minutes   **SLOW COOK:** 5½ hours (low) or 2¾ hours (high) + 30 minutes (high)

3	14½-ounce cans reduced-sodium chicken broth
1	pound fresh white button mushrooms, quartered
2	cups regular pearled barley
2	medium leeks, sliced (⅔ cup)
1	teaspoon dried leaf thyme, crushed
¼	teaspoon ground black pepper
4	ounces reduced-fat cream cheese (Neufchâtel)
1	12-ounce package soft silken-style tofu (fresh bean curd)
1	pound asparagus, trimmed and cut into bite-size pieces
½	cup snipped fresh basil
¼	cup finely shredded Parmesan cheese

1. In a 6-quart slow cooker combine the broth, mushrooms, barley, leeks, thyme, and pepper. Cover and cook on low-heat setting for 5½ hours or on high-heat setting for 2¾ hours.

2. If using low-heat setting, turn to high-heat setting. In a blender or food processor combine the cream cheese and tofu. Cover and blend or process until smooth. Stir the asparagus and cream cheese mixture into the cooker. Cover and cook for 30 minutes more. Stir in basil and top with Parmesan. **Makes 8 servings.**

PER SERVING: 281 cal., 6 g fat (3 g sat. fat), 12 mg chol., 458 mg sodium, 46 g carb., 9 g fiber, 14 g pro.

cook smart There are two basic types of tofu: water-packed and silken. Water-packed tofu holds together better when cut and is best used for stir-frying, grilling, and sautéing. Silken tofu, which this recipe uses, can be blended into creamy smoothies, sauces, and dips and adds a rich consistency. It comes in soft to extra-firm texture and may be located on the shelf in your supermarket rather than in the refrigerated or produce section.

If you like more kick, add chili powder to the rice mixture before cooking and Monterey Jack cheese with jalapeño peppers in place of the plain cheese.

chili bean-stuffed peppers

PREP: 20 minutes   **SLOW COOK:** 6 hours (low) or 3 hours (high)

4   small to medium green, red, or yellow sweet peppers
1   15-ounce can vegetarian baked beans, undrained
1   cup cooked converted rice
1   15-ounce can no-salt-added tomato sauce
⅓   cup finely chopped onion (1 small)
¾   cup shredded Monterey Jack cheese (3 ounces)
     Chili powder (optional)

1. Remove tops, seeds, and membranes from sweet peppers. Chop enough tops to make ⅓ cup; set aside. If necessary, cut a thin slice from the bottom of each pepper so it will stand flat.

2. In a medium bowl stir together beans and cooked rice; spoon into peppers. Pour tomato sauce into a 4½- to 6-quart slow cooker; stir in onion and the reserved ⅓ cup chopped pepper. Place filled peppers, filling sides up, in cooker.

3. Cover and cook on low-heat setting for 6 to 6½ hours or on high-heat setting for 3 to 3½ hours.

4. To serve, transfer peppers to dinner plates and, if desired, cut in half. Spoon tomato mixture over peppers. Sprinkle with cheese and, if desired, chili powder. **Makes 4 servings.**

PER SERVING: 314 cal., 7 g fat (4 g sat. fat), 19 mg chol., 522 mg sodium, 47 g carb., 9 g fiber, 13 g pro.

MEATLESS

This Sicilian-style pasta dish is so packed with vegetables, you don't really need to serve anything else with it—although a fennel and orange salad dressed with olive oil and vinegar makes a refreshing side.

pasta with eggplant sauce

PREP: 25 minutes **SLOW COOK:** 7 hours (low) or 3½ hours (high)

1	eggplant
2	14½-ounce cans no-salt-added diced tomatoes, undrained
1	6-ounce can Italian-style tomato paste
1	4-ounce can (drained weight) sliced mushrooms, drained
½	cup chopped onion (1 medium)
¼	cup dry red wine
¼	cup water
1½	teaspoons dried oregano, crushed
2	cloves garlic, minced
⅓	cup pitted Kalamata olives or ripe olives, sliced
2	tablespoons snipped fresh Italian (flat-leaf) parsley
	Ground black pepper
4	cups hot cooked whole grain penne pasta
3	tablespoons grated or shredded Parmesan cheese
2	tablespoons pine nuts, toasted (see tip, page 23) (optional)

1. If desired, peel eggplant; cut eggplant into 1-inch pieces. In a 3½- to 5-quart slow cooker combine eggplant, tomatoes, tomato paste, mushrooms, onion, wine, the water, oregano, and garlic.

2. Cover and cook on low-heat setting for 7 to 8 hours or on high-heat setting for 3½ to 4 hours.

3. Stir in olives and parsley. Season to taste with pepper. Serve over hot cooked pasta. Sprinkle with cheese and, if desired, pine nuts. **Makes 6 servings.**

PER SERVING: 249 cal., 3 g fat (1 g sat. fat), 2 mg chol., 520 mg sodium, 46 g carb., 6 g fiber, 9 g pro.

● LOW CALORIE ◉ HIGH FIBER ● VEGETARIAN

A small amount of bottled mole sauce and a teaspoon of unsweetened cocoa powder give this meatless dish its "mole" credentials.

black bean and rice mole tacos

PREP: 25 minutes   **SLOW COOK:** 6 hours (low) or 3 hours (high) + 1 hour (high)

2 15-ounce cans no-salt-added black beans, rinsed and drained
2 medium red sweet peppers, cut into bite -size pieces
1 14½-ounce can vegetable broth
1 cup chopped onion
1 fresh jalapeño chile pepper, seeded and minced (see tip, page 14)
2 teaspoons ground ancho chile pepper
1 teaspoon ground cumin
1 14½-ounce can diced tomatoes
½ cup instant brown rice
¼ cup bottled mole sauce
1 teaspoon unsweetened cocoa powder
½ teaspoon salt
16 6-inch corn tortillas, warmed
2 cups shredded green cabbage
1 avocado, halved, seeded, peeled, and chopped
½ cup snipped fresh cilantro
   Lime wedges

1. In a 3½- to 4-quart slow cooker combine beans, red sweet peppers, broth, onion, jalapeño, ground ancho chile pepper, and cumin. Cover and cook on low-heat setting for 6 to 8 hours or on high-heat setting for 3 to 4 hours.

2. If using low-heat setting, turn to high-heat setting. Stir in the tomatoes, brown rice, mole sauce, cocoa powder, and salt. Cover and cook 1 hour more or until rice is tender.

3. Serve in corn tortillas topped with cabbage, avocado, and cilantro. Pass lime wedges. **Makes 8 servings.**

PER SERVING: 255 cal., 9 g fat (1 g sat. fat), 0 mg chol, 453 mg sodium, 35 g carb., 10 g fiber, 12 g pro.

cook smart Corn tortillas have almost half the calories and about 5 fewer grams of fat than flour tortillas, making them a health-smart choice for tacos. Plus, the corn flavor meshes well with the black beans and mole in this recipe.

An old-fashioned favorite gets a vegetarian twist with lentils substituted for ground beef. Your family might not even notice the healthful upgrade.

sloppy veggie sandwiches

PREP: 20 minutes   **SLOW COOK:** 3½ hours (high)

1	cup chopped carrots (2 medium)
1	cup chopped celery (2 stalks)
⅔	cup brown lentils, rinsed and drained
⅔	cup uncooked regular brown rice
½	cup chopped onion (1 medium)
2	tablespoons packed brown sugar
2	tablespoons yellow mustard
½	teaspoon salt
1	clove garlic, minced
⅛	to ¼ teaspoon cayenne pepper
2	14½-ounce cans vegetable or chicken broth
1	15-ounce can tomato sauce
2	tablespoons apple cider vinegar
8	whole wheat hamburger buns or French-style rolls, split and toasted

1. In a 3½- or 4-quart slow cooker combine carrots, celery, lentils, brown rice, onion, brown sugar, mustard, salt, garlic, and cayenne pepper. Stir in broth.

2. Cover and cook on high-heat setting for 3 to 3½ hours. Stir in tomato sauce and vinegar. Cover and cook on high-heat setting for 30 minutes more.

3. To serve, spoon lentil mixture into toasted buns. **Makes 8 servings.**

PER SERVING: 261 cal., 4 g fat (1 g sat. fat), 0 mg chol., 1,036 mg sodium, 50 g carb., 8 g fiber, 11 g pro.

Cumin, paprika, and cayenne pepper infuse this broth-based stew with kicky flavor. All you need is a slice of chewy whole grain bread to soak up the juices.

garbanzo bean stew

PREP: 20 minutes   **SLOW COOK:** 9 hours (low) or 4½ hours (high)

3	15-ounce cans no-salt-added garbanzo beans (chickpeas), rinsed and drained
1	pound red-skin potatoes, cut into ¾-inch pieces
1	14½-ounce can no-salt-added diced tomatoes, undrained
¾	cup chopped red sweet pepper (1 medium)
½	cup chopped onion (1 medium)
3	cloves garlic, minced
1	teaspoon ground cumin
½	teaspoon paprika
¼	teaspoon cayenne pepper
2	14½-ounce cans vegetable broth or chicken broth

1. In a 5- to 6-quart slow cooker combine beans, potatoes, tomatoes, sweet pepper, onion, garlic, cumin, paprika, and cayenne pepper. Pour broth over mixture in cooker.

2. Cover and cook on low-heat setting for 9 to 10 hours or on high-heat setting for 4½ to 5 hours. **Makes 6 servings.**

PER SERVING: 293 cal., 3 g fat (0 g sat. fat), 0 mg chol., 590 mg sodium, 53 g carb., 12 g fiber, 14 g pro.

Crisp, crunchy Parmesan toast makes a nicely contrasting accompaniment to the chunky mélange of vegetables and cannellini beans.

ratatouille with white beans on parmesan toast

PREP: 30 minutes   **SLOW COOK:** 4½ hours (low) or 2 hours (high)

4	cups cubed, peeled (if desired) eggplant
1	15- to 15½-ounce can no-salt-added cannellini beans (white kidney beans), rinsed and drained
1	14½-ounce can fire-roasted diced tomatoes, undrained
1½	cups coarsely chopped yellow summer squash or zucchini
1	8-ounce can no-salt-added tomato sauce
¾	cup coarsely chopped red or green sweet pepper (1 medium)
½	cup finely chopped onion (1 medium)
2	cloves garlic, chopped
¼	teaspoon ground black pepper Pinch salt
2	tablespoons snipped fresh basil
8	½-inch-thick slices baguette-style French bread, toasted*
2	tablespoons finely shredded Parmesan cheese

1. In a 3½- or 4-quart slow cooker combine eggplant, beans, tomatoes, squash, tomato sauce, sweet pepper, onion, garlic, black pepper, and salt.

2. Cover and cook on low-heat setting for 4½ to 5 hours or on high-heat setting for 2 to 2½ hours.

3. Stir basil into mixture in cooker. Serve eggplant mixture with bread slices; sprinkle with cheese. **Makes 4 servings.**

*Tip: To toast bread slices, preheat broiler. Brush one side of each bread slice with some of 1 tablespoon olive oil. Place bread slices, oil sides up, on a baking sheet. Broil 3 to 4 inches from heat about 15 seconds or until toasted (watch carefully to avoid burning). Sprinkle bread slices with some of 2 tablespoons finely shredded Parmesan cheese. Broil about 15 seconds longer or until cheese is melted.

PER SERVING: 395 cal., 7 g fat (2 g sat. fat), 4 mg chol., 951 mg sodium, 72 g carb., 14 g fiber, 19 g pro.

● HIGH FIBER ● VEGETARIAN

Use a little bit of every kind of suggested vegetable—cauliflower, onion, and multicolor sweet peppers—for the most color and nutrition.

new delhi vegetable curry with whole wheat couscous

PREP: 30 minutes   **SLOW COOK:** 6 hours (low) or 3 hours (high) + 5 minutes   **STAND:** 5 minutes

1½   cups sweet potatoes, peeled and cut into ½-inch pieces (2 medium)
5   cups assorted vegetables, such as cauliflower florets, onion wedges, and/or 1-inch pieces red or green sweet pepper
1   cup canned no-salt-added garbanzo beans (chickpeas), rinsed and drained
1¾   cups reduced-sodium vegetable broth
2   teaspoons curry powder
2   teaspoons grated fresh ginger
1   clove garlic, minced
½   teaspoon salt
⅛   teaspoon cayenne pepper
2   cups fresh baby spinach leaves (5 ounces)
1   cup unsweetened light coconut milk
¼   cup golden raisins
⅔   cup uncooked whole wheat couscous
⅛   teaspoon salt
¾   cup boiling water
½   teaspoon olive oil
¼   cup plain nonfat yogurt
¼   cup snipped fresh cilantro

1. In a 4- to 5-quart slow cooker combine sweet potatoes, vegetables, and beans. In a medium bowl stir together broth, curry powder, ginger, garlic, the ½ teaspoon salt, and the cayenne pepper. Pour over mixture in cooker.

2. Cover and cook on low-heat setting for 6 to 7 hours or on high-heat setting for 3 to 3½ hours. Stir spinach, coconut milk, and raisins into cooker. Cover and cook for 5 to 10 minutes more or until spinach is wilted.

3. Meanwhile, in a small bowl combine couscous and the ⅛ teaspoon salt; pour the boiling water and oil over mixture. Let stand for 5 minutes.

4. Serve vegetable mixture over couscous. Top each serving with yogurt and cilantro. **Makes 4 servings.**

PER SERVING: 394 cal., 6 g fat (2 g sat. fat), 0 mg chol., 710 mg sodium, 75 g carb., 14 g fiber, 14 g pro.

Rustic and rich in deep flavors, this hearty chili satisfies big appetites with complete vegetarian protein from the combination of rice and beans.

sassy bean and brown rice chili

PREP: 25 minutes   **SLOW COOK:** 7 hours (low) or 3½ hours (high)

2	cups reduced-sodium vegetable broth
1	16-ounce jar picante sauce
2	cups water
1	15-ounce can no-salt-added pinto or red kidney beans, rinsed and drained
1	15-ounce can no-salt-added black beans, rinsed and drained
1	15-ounce can no-salt-added garbanzo beans (chickpeas), rinsed and drained
¾	cup uncooked brown rice
½	cup chopped onion (1 medium)
1	4-ounce can diced green chiles, undrained
2	tablespoons chili powder
1	tablespoon unsweetened cocoa powder
2	cloves garlic, minced
⅓	cup plain nonfat yogurt
⅓	cup crumbled Cotija cheese or shredded reduced-fat Monterey Jack cheese
¼	cup roasted pumpkin seeds (pepitas)

1. In a 3½-or 4-quart quart slow cooker combine broth, picante sauce, the water, pinto beans, black beans, garbanzo beans, uncooked rice, onion, chiles, chili powder, cocoa powder, and garlic.

2. Cover and cook on low-heat setting for 7 to 8 hours or on high-heat setting for 3½ to 4 hours.

3. To serve, top each serving with yogurt and sprinkle with cheese and pumpkin seeds. **Makes 6 servings.**

PER SERVING: 415 cal., 11 g fat (1 g sat. fat), 11 mg chol., 937 mg sodium, 61 g carb., 12 g fiber, 22 g pro.

Farro is an ancient grain belonging to the wheat family. It's often confused with spelt (see page 181), but they are different grains. Farro has a dense, chewy texture and a rich, nutty flavor.

mediterranean kale and cannellini stew with farro

PREP: 20 minutes   **SLOW COOK:** 3 hours (high)

4 cups reduced-sodium vegetable broth or reduced-sodium chicken broth
1 14½-ounce can no-salt-added fire-roasted tomatoes
1 cup farro, rinsed, or kamut
1 cup coarsely chopped onion (1 large)
2 medium carrots, halved lengthwise and thinly sliced crosswise
1 cup coarsely chopped celery (2 stalks)
4 cloves garlic, crushed
½ teaspoon crushed red pepper
¼ teaspoon salt
4 cups coarsely chopped fresh green kale or Swiss chard
1 15-ounce can no-salt-added cannellini beans (white kidney beans), rinsed and drained
3 tablespoons fresh lemon juice
½ cup crumbled feta cheese (2 ounces)
   Snipped fresh basil or parsley

1. In a 3½- or 4-quart slow cooker combine broth, tomatoes, farro, onion, carrots, celery, garlic, crushed red pepper, and salt.

2. Cover and cook on high-heat setting about 2 hours or until farro is tender but still chewy. Stir in kale, beans, and lemon juice. Cover and cook for 1 hour more.

3. To serve, sprinkle each serving with cheese and basil or parsley. **Makes 6 servings.**

PER SERVING: 274 cal., 4 g fat (2 g sat. fat), 11 mg chol., 691 mg sodium, 46 g carb., 9 g fiber, 14 g pro.

cook smart Kale is the new darling in the health-food section—and Swiss chard is also no stranger to those who are interested in healthful eating. Kale is high in vitamins A, C, and K. And including it regularly in your diet can help ward off heart disease and cancer due to the antioxidant and anti-inflammatory properties. If you can't find either of these greens, spinach will pinch-hit just fine.

Two kinds of corn give this soup a rich consistency and well-balanced texture.

cha-cha corn chowder

PREP: 15 minutes   **SLOW COOK:** 6 hours (low) or 3 hours (high)

3	medium round red potatoes, finely chopped (1 pound)
2	14¾-ounce cans cream-style corn
1	14½-ounce can vegetable broth
1	clove garlic, minced
1	11-ounce can whole kernel corn with sweet peppers, drained
1	4-ounce can diced green chile peppers, undrained
¼	teaspoon ground black pepper
	Cracked black pepper (optional)
	Saltine crackers (optional)

1. In a 3½- or 4-quart slow cooker combine potatoes, cream-style corn, broth, garlic, corn with sweet peppers, undrained green chile peppers, and ground black pepper.

2. Cover and cook on low-heat setting for 6 to 8 hours or on high-heat setting for 3 to 4 hours. If desired, top each serving with cracked black pepper and/or serve with crackers. **Makes 6 servings.**

PER SERVING: 202 cal., 1 g fat (0 g. sat. fat), 1 mg chol., 898 mg sodium, 49 g carb., 5 g fiber, 5 g pro.

● LOW CALORIE   ◐ HIGH FIBER   ◐ VEGETARIAN

You can use either butternut or acorn squash in this stew. Butternut squash will have a slightly firmer texture after a long cooking time than the acorn squash.

vegetable stew with cornmeal dumplings

PREP: 25 minutes   **SLOW COOK:** 8 hours (low) or 4 hours (high) + 50 minutes (high)

3 cups chopped, peeled butternut or acorn squash (1 pound)

2 cups sliced fresh mushrooms

2 14½-ounce cans diced tomatoes, undrained

1 15-ounce can Great Northern beans, rinsed and drained

1 cup water

4 cloves garlic, minced

1 teaspoon dried Italian seasoning, crushed

¼ teaspoon ground black pepper

½ cup all-purpose flour

⅓ cup cornmeal

2 tablespoons grated Parmesan cheese

1 tablespoon snipped fresh Italian parsley

1 teaspoon baking powder

¼ teaspoon salt

1 egg, lightly beaten

2 tablespoons milk

2 tablespoons vegetable oil

1 9-ounce package frozen Italian green beans or cut green beans
Paprika

1. In a 3½- or 4-quart slow cooker combine squash and mushrooms. Stir in tomatoes, Great Northern beans, the water, garlic, Italian seasoning, and pepper.

2. Cover and cook on low-heat setting for 8 to 10 hours or on high-heat setting for 4 to 5 hours.

3. Shortly before serving, for dumplings, in a medium bowl, stir together flour, cornmeal, cheese, parsley, baking powder, and salt. In a small bowl combine egg, milk, and oil. Stir egg mixture into flour mixture just until combined.

4. If using low-heat setting, turn to high-heat setting. Stir in frozen green beans. Drop dumpling dough by tablespoons on top of mixture in cooker; sprinkle with paprika. Cover and cook for 50 minutes more, leaving the lid on during the entire time. **Makes 6 servings.**

PER SERVING: 288 cal., 7 g fat (2 g sat. fat), 37 mg chol., 442 mg sodium, 45 g carb., 7 g fiber, 12 g pro.

Use your favorite flavorful broth with this bounty of fresh veggies—tomatoes and carrots, celery, sweet pepper, fennel, or onion. Serve with crusty whole grain bread and hummus to round out the meal.

garden tomato soup

PREP: 25 minutes   **COOK:** 6 hours (low) or 3 hours (high)

2   **pounds roma tomatoes, chopped**
2   **14½-ounce cans vegetable broth**
2   **cups finely chopped assorted vegetables (such as carrot, celery, sweet pepper, fennel, and/ or onion)**
1   **6-ounce can tomato paste**
1   **to 2 teaspoons sugar**

1. In a 3½- or 4-quart slow cooker combine tomatoes, broth, vegetables, tomato paste, and sugar.

2. Cover and cook on low-heat setting for 6 to 8 hours or on high-heat setting for 3 to 4 hours. **Makes 8 servings.**

PER SERVING: 61 cal., 1 g fat (0 g sat. fat), 0 mg chol., 372 mg sodium, 12 g carb., 3 g fiber, 3 g pro.

cook smart Even if you aren't committed to a completely meatless diet, reducing your meat intake by choosing a meatless meal a couple times each week can help reduce your risk of cancer, diabetes, and certain cancers.

MEATLESS

A popular appetizer makes a main-dish leap in this earthy soup. If you like hummus as a snack, you'll love a bowl of this soup for supper.

thick hummus-style soup

PREP: 35 minutes   **SLOW COOK:** 10 hours (low) or 5 hours (high)   **BAKE:** 12 minutes at 300°F

1	pound dried garbanzo beans (chickpeas)
8	cups vegetable broth or reduced-sodium chicken broth
6	cloves garlic, minced
1	tablespoon ground cumin
1	teaspoon ground coriander
1	teaspoon ground turmeric
½	teaspoon salt
1	6-ounce carton plain fat-free Greek yogurt
⅓	cup tahini
⅓	cup lemon juice
⅓	cup snipped fresh Italian (flat-leaf) parsley
1	to 2 whole grain pita bread rounds
1	tablespoon olive oil
1¼	cups chopped red sweet pepper (1 large)
	Toasted sesame seeds (see tip, page 23) (optional)

1. Rinse beans. In a large saucepan or Dutch oven combine beans and enough water to cover. Bring to boiling. Boil, uncovered, for 10 minutes. Drain and rinse beans. Place in a 4- to 5-quart slow cooker. Add broth, garlic, cumin, coriander, turmeric, and salt.

2. Cover and cook on low-heat setting for 10 to 12 hours or on high-heat setting for 5 to 6 hours.

3. Stir yogurt, tahini, and lemon juice into mixture in cooker. Using an immersion blender,* carefully blend soup. Stir in parsley.

4. Meanwhile, preheat oven to 300°F. Chop enough pita bread into ¼- to ½-inch pieces to equal 2 cups; toss with olive oil. Spread in a shallow baking pan; bake for 12 to 13 minutes or until crisp, stirring once.

5. Serve soup topped with sweet pepper, pita bread pieces, and, if desired, sesame seeds. **Makes 8 servings.**

*Tip: If you don't have an immersion blender, cool slightly and process in batches in a regular blender.

PER SERVING: 351 cal., 11 g fat (1 g sat. fat), 0 mg chol., 768 mg sodium, 47 g carb., 12 g fiber, 18 g pro.

Serve this soup with pappadum (crisp Indian lentil crackers) and a cooling raita, a yogurt condiment. To make raita, stir together yogurt, chopped cucumber, and fresh mint, and a pinch each of cumin and cayenne.

coconut-ginger lentil soup

PREP: 20 minutes **SLOW COOK:** 5 hours (low) or 2½ hours (high) + 30 minutes (high)

3	14½-ounce cans vegetable broth
2	cups dried red lentils (12 ounces), rinsed
1½	cups chopped celery
1½	cups chopped carrots
1½	cups chopped onions
2	tablespoons grated fresh ginger
2	teaspoons curry powder
3	cloves garlic, minced
½	teaspoon ground cumin
½	teaspoon ground coriander
½	teaspoon ground turmeric
¼	teaspoon ground cinnamon
1	14-ounce can unsweetened light coconut milk
	Thinly sliced green onions (optional)
	Snipped fresh cilantro (optional)
	Fresh serrano pepper, seeded and minced (see tip, page 14) (optional)
	Lime wedges (optional)

1. In a 5- to 6-quart slow cooker combine the broth, lentils, celery, carrots, onions, ginger, curry powder, garlic, cumin, coriander, turmeric, and cinnamon.

2. Cover and cook on low-heat setting for 5 to 6 hours or on high-heat setting for 2½ to 3 hours. If using low-heat setting, turn to high-heat setting. Stir in the coconut milk, cover and cook 30 minutes more. If desired, serve with green onions, cilantro, serrano pepper, and/or lime wedges. **Makes 8 servings.**

PER SERVING: 239 cal., 4 g fat (3 g sat. fat), 0 mg chol., 568 mg sodium, 39 g carb., 16 g fiber, 14 g pro.

summer
slow cooker

When it's hot outside, saucy barbecue and cool, crisp, lighter foods with lots of veggies—like these recipes—hit the spot.

A sprightly citrus mayo and slices of creamy avocado add rich flavor to this tasty sandwich.

cuban shredded beef sandwich

PREP: 20 minutes   **SLOW COOK:** 9 hours (low) or 4½ hours (high)

1	teaspoon dried oregano, crushed
1	teaspoon ground cumin
½	teaspoon salt
½	teaspoon ground black pepper
⅛	teaspoon ground allspice
1	2- to 2½-pound boneless beef chuck arm pot roast, trimmed of fat
	Nonstick cooking spray
1	cup sliced onion
1	cup sliced green sweet pepper
4	cloves garlic, minced
2	bay leaves
¼	cup orange juice
¼	cup lime juice
1	avocado, sliced
1	recipe Citrus Mayo
6	kaiser rolls, split and toasted

1. In a small bowl combine the oregano, cumin, salt, black pepper, and allspice. Press spice mixture onto both sides of the roast. Coat a large nonstick skillet with cooking spray; heat over medium-high heat. Add roast; cook until light brown on both sides, turning once.

2. Meanwhile, coat a 3½- or 4-quart slow cooker with cooking spray. Layer onion, green pepper, garlic, and bay leaves in cooker. Pour orange juice and lime juice over vegetables. If necessary, cut roast to fit in cooker. Place roast on top of vegetables. Cover and cook on low-heat setting for 9 to 10 hours or on high-heat setting for 4½ to 5 hours.

3. Using a slotted spoon, transfer meat to a cutting board. Strain cooking liquid. Remove and discard bay leaves; reserve onion and green pepper. Using two forks, pull meat apart into shreds; return to cooker. Skim fat from cooking liquid. Stir in reserved onion and pepper and ½ cup cooking liquid into cooker. If desired, add additional cooking liquid to the cooker. Discard remaining cooking liquid.

4. To serve, divide meat among the bottom halves of the rolls. Top with avocado. Spread about 2 teaspoons Citrus Mayo on cut sides of each of the roll tops. Add roll tops to sandwiches. **Makes 6 servings.**

Citrus Mayo: In a small bowl combine ¼ cup reduced-fat mayonnaise, ½ teaspoon finely shredded orange peel, 1 teaspoon orange juice, ¼ teaspoon finely shredded lime peel, ½ teaspoon lime juice, ⅛ teaspoon salt, and a pinch of ground pepper. Whisk until smooth.

PER SERVING: 383 cal., 12 g fat (3 g sat. fat), 64 mg chol., 702 mg sodium, 40 g carb., 4 g fiber, 28 g pro.

The gravy for this fork-tender brisket is made from a tantalizing blend of beer, chili sauce, brown sugar, and seasonings, which goes well alongside simple roasted potato wedges.

brisket with ale bbq sauce

PREP: 25 minutes **SLOW COOK:** 10 hours (low) or 5 hours (high)

1   3- to 4-pound boneless beef
    brisket
2   medium onions, thinly sliced and
    separated into rings
1   bay leaf
1   12-ounce can beer
¼   cup chili sauce
2   tablespoons packed brown sugar
1   clove garlic, minced
½   teaspoon dried thyme, crushed
¼   teaspoon salt
¼   teaspoon ground black pepper
2   tablespoons cornstarch
2   tablespoons cold water

1. Trim fat from meat. If necessary, cut meat to fit into a 3½- or 4-quart slow cooker. In cooker combine onions and bay leaf; add meat. In a medium bowl combine beer, chili sauce, brown sugar, garlic, thyme, salt, and pepper. Pour over meat.

2. Cover and cook on low-heat setting for 10 to 12 hours or high-heat setting for 5 to 6 hours.

3. Using a slotted spoon, transfer meat and onions to a serving platter. Slice meat across the grain; cover and keep warm. Discard bay leaf.

4. For sauce, pour enough of the cooking liquid into a 4-cup glass measuring cup to equal 2½ cups; skim off fat. Discard the remaining cooking liquid. In a medium saucepan combine cornstarch and the cold water; stir in the 2½ cups cooking liquid. Cook and stir over medium heat until thickened and bubbly. Cook and stir for 2 minutes more. Serve meat and onions with sauce. **Makes 10 servings.**

PER SERVING: 227 cal., 7 g fat (2 g sat. fat), 78 mg chol., 242 mg sodium, 8 g carb., 1 g fiber, 30 g pro.

cook smart Brisket may conjure up images of greasy-spoon BBQ joints, but it's actually quite lean when prepared the right way. Most of the fat is located in an easy-to-remove layer on the top of the roast. The meat itself is quite lean. Cooking it low and slow in the slow cooker makes it fork tender and allows it to soak up all the flavorful juices.

Coleslaw adds a finishing crunchy touch to flavorful shredded pork shoulder sandwiches served on whole grain buns.

bbq pulled pork sliders

PREP: 30 minutes   **SLOW COOK:** 9 hours (low) or 4½ hours (high) + 1 hour (low)

- 1 2½- to 3-pound boneless pork shoulder roast
- 1 cup chopped onion (1 large)
- ¾ cup chopped green sweet pepper (1 medium)
- 1 teaspoon dried thyme, crushed
- ½ teaspoon dried rosemary, crushed
- ½ cup chicken broth
- 1 cup balsamic vinegar
- ¾ cup ketchup
- ⅓ cup packed brown sugar
- ¼ cup honey
- 1 tablespoon Worcestershire sauce
- 1 tablespoon Dijon mustard
- 1 clove garlic, minced
- ½ teaspoon ground black pepper
- ¼ teaspoon salt
- 20 cocktail-size hamburger buns or small round dinner rolls, split and toasted
  Deli coleslaw
  Coarsely chopped sweet or dill pickles

1. Trim fat from meat. If necessary, cut meat to fit into a 3½- or 4-quart slow cooker. In cooker combine onion and sweet pepper. Add meat; sprinkle with thyme and rosemary. Pour broth over meat.

2. Cover and cook on low-heat setting for 9 to 10 hours or on high-heat setting for 4½ to 5 hours.

3. Meanwhile, for barbecue sauce, in a medium saucepan combine vinegar, ketchup, brown sugar, honey, Worcestershire sauce, mustard, garlic, black pepper, and salt. Bring to boiling; reduce heat. Simmer, uncovered, for 20 to 25 minutes or until sauce is slightly thickened, stirring occasionally.

4. Transfer meat to a cutting board. Using two forks, pull meat apart into shreds, discarding fat. Strain vegetable mixture, discarding liquid. Return shredded meat and strained vegetables to cooker. Stir in barbecue sauce. If using high-heat setting, turn to low-heat setting. Cover and cook for 1 hour.

5. To serve, spoon meat mixture onto bun bottoms. Top with coleslaw and choppped pickles. Add bun tops. **Makes 20 sliders.**

PER SLIDER: 320 cal., 14 g fat (4 g sat. fat), 44 mg chol., 487 mg sodium, 34 g carb., 1 g fiber, 13 g pro.

With the flavors of Vietnamese banh mi, this dish will liven up any lunch or dinner. Evenly distribute the ingredients in each wrap so every bite takes in all of the sweet, sour, and spicy flavors.

vietnamese pork

PREP: 25 minutes   **SLOW COOK:** 10 hours (low) or 5 hours (high)

2	fresh jalapeño chile peppers (see tip, page 14)
1	2½- to 3-pound boneless pork shoulder roast
2	tablespoons packed brown sugar
½	teaspoon ground black pepper
1	medium onion, cut into thin wedges
2	cloves garlic, minced
¼	cup water
2	tablespoons fish sauce
2	tablespoons lime juice
8	whole wheat flour tortillas, warmed (see tip, page 70)
4	cups mesclun mix
1	cup halved cucumber slices
1	recipe Pickled Carrots
¼	cup snipped fresh cilantro

1. Cut one of the jalapeño peppers in half lengthwise. Thinly slice the remaining jalapeño pepper; wrap and chill the sliced pepper until ready to serve.

2. Trim fat from meat. If necessary, cut meat to fit into a 3½- or 4-quart slow cooker. For rub, in a small bowl stir together brown sugar and black pepper. Sprinkle rub evenly over meat; rub in with your fingers. Place meat in the cooker. Add halved jalapeño pepper, onion, and garlic. In a small bowl stir together the water, fish sauce, and lime juice. Pour over mixture in cooker.

3. Cover and cook on low-heat setting for 10 to 12 hours or on high-heat setting for 5 to 6 hours.

4. Using a slotted spoon, remove meat and onion from cooker; discard cooking liquid. Using two forks, pull meat apart into shreds. Stir onion into shredded meat.

5. For each serving, spoon ⅔ cup of the shredded meat mixture onto a tortilla. Top with mesclun mix, cucumber, Pickled Carrots, cilantro, and sliced jalapeño pepper. **Makes 8 servings.**

Pickled Carrots: In a nonreactive bowl stir together ½ cup warm water, 2 tablespoons white vinegar, 1 tablespoon sugar, and ½ teaspoon salt. Add 2 carrots, cut into thin bite-size strips (1 cup). Cover and chill for 8 hours before serving. Store in the refrigerator for up to 1 week.

PER SERVING: 362 cal., 7 g fat (2 g sat. fat), 85 mg chol., 966 mg sodium, 36 g carb., 3 g fiber, 37 g pro.

With crisp sweet peppers, water chestnuts, and pineapple, this dish tastes pretty much like the popular Chinese restaurant staple—without the high-fat sauce.

sweet-and-sour pork

PREP: 30 minutes   **SLOW COOK:** 7 hours (low) or 3½ hours (high)

2   pounds boneless pork shoulder roast, trimmed of fat and cut into 1-inch pieces
2   teaspoons olive oil
1   20-ounce can pineapple chunks (juice pack)
1   green sweet pepper, cut into 1-inch pieces
1   red sweet pepper, cut into 1-inch pieces
1   large onion, cut into thin wedges
1   8-ounce can sliced water chestnuts, drained
¼   cup rice vinegar
3   tablespoons ketchup
3   tablespoons reduced-sodium soy sauce
3   tablespoons quick-cooking tapioca, crushed
2   tablespoons packed brown sugar
2   cloves garlic, minced
2   teaspoons grated fresh ginger
½   teaspoon sesame oil
1   cup sugar snap peas, trimmed
3   cups hot cooked brown rice
⅓   cup slivered green onion

1. In a very large skillet brown pork on all sides in hot oil. Drain fat. Transfer pork to a 3½- or 4-quart slow cooker.

2. Drain pineapple chunks, reserving ⅓ cup of the juice; set pineapple chunks aside.

3. Add green pepper, red pepper, onion, and water chestnuts to cooker. In a medium bowl whisk together the reserved ⅓ cup pineapple juice, rice vinegar, ketchup, soy sauce, tapioca, brown sugar, garlic, ginger, and sesame oil. Pour over all in cooker.

4. Cover and cook on low-heat setting for 7 to 8 hours or on high-heat setting for 3½ to 4 hours.

5. Stir in sugar snap peas and reserved pineapple chunks. Serve over hot cooked rice. Sprinkle with green onions. **Makes 6 servings.**

PER SERVING: 402 cal., 8 g fat (2 g sat. fat), 61 mg chol., 443 mg sodium, 55 g carb., 4 g fiber, 24 g pro.

● LOW CALORIE

This dish delivers double the pleasure for almost no effort. The meat needs no prepping before going into the slow cooker, and the Asian slaw adds a pleasing freshness and crunch that's hard to resist.

teriyaki pork with asian slaw

PREP: 25 minutes   **SLOW COOK:** 5 hours (low) or 2½ hours (high)

2	12-ounce pork tenderloins
½	cup reduced-sodium soy sauce
¼	cup rice vinegar
3	tablespoons packed brown sugar
2	tablespoons canola oil
2	teaspoons grated fresh ginger
2	cloves garlic, minced
¼	teaspoon ground black pepper
	Toasted sesame seeds (optional)
1	recipe Asian Slaw

1. Trim fat from meat. Place meat in a 3½- or 4-quart slow cooker. In a small bowl whisk together soy sauce, vinegar, brown sugar, oil, ginger, garlic, and pepper. Pour over meat.

2. Cover and cook on low-heat setting for 5 to 6 hours or on high-heat setting for 2½ to 3 hours.

3. Transfer meat to a cutting board, reserving cooking liquid. Cut meat into ½-inch slices.

4. To serve, drizzle meat with cooking liquid. If desired, sprinkle with sesame seeds. Serve with Asian Slaw. **Makes 8 servings.**

Asian Slaw: In a bowl combine 5 cups shredded napa cabbage; 1 medium yellow sweet pepper, cut into bite-size strips; ½ cup shredded carrot (1 medium); ½ cup snow pea pods sliced lengthwise; and ¼ cup sliced green onions. In a screw-top jar combine 3 tablespoons rice vinegar, 2 tablespoons canola oil, 1 tablespoon toasted sesame oil, 1 tablespoon reduced-sodium soy sauce, ¼ teaspoon salt, and ¼ teaspoon ground black pepper. Shake well. Drizzle dressing over vegetables and toss to coat.

PER SERVING: 239 cal., 11 g fat (1 g sat. fat), 55 mg chol., 731 mg sodium, 14 g carb., 2 g fiber, 21 g pro.

cook smart Pork tenderloin is as low in fat as chicken breast, making it a great choice for low-calorie cooking. Three ounces roasted pork tenderloin has about 120 calories and just 3 grams of fat. Plus, if you think low-fat meat usually turns out dry, pork tenderloin will surprise you with an ultramoist result.

Update your comfort-food dishes with this colorful one-dish dinner. A creamy combination of turkey, pasta, and dried cherries is served on a bed of baby spinach and topped with almonds and feta cheese.

turkey orzo with dried cherries and feta cheese

PREP: 15 minutes   **SLOW COOK:** 2 hours (low)

Nonstick cooking spray
1¾ cups whole wheat orzo
1½ pounds turkey breast, cut into
   ½-inch cubes
2¾ cups reduced-sodium chicken
   broth
1¼ cups coarsely chopped red onions
½ cup dried cherries
2 tablespoons lemon juice
3 cloves garlic, minced
½ teaspoon ground black pepper
¼ teaspoon salt
6 cups lightly packed baby spinach
½ cup feta cheese (2 ounces)
¼ cup chopped almonds
1 tablespoon snipped fresh parsley

1. Coat a large skillet with cooking spray. Heat over medium heat. Add orzo; cook and stir for 3 to 4 minutes or until golden.

2. Coat a 3½- or 4-quart slow cooker with cooking spray. In cooker combine orzo, turkey, broth, onion, cherries, lemon juice, garlic, pepper, and salt.

3. Cover and cook on low-heat setting for 2 hours.

4. Serve turkey mixture on top of spinach. Sprinkle with cheese, almonds, and parsley. **Makes 8 servings.**

PER SERVING: 334 cal., 5 g fat (2 g sat. fat), 61 mg chol., 451 mg sodium, 41 g carb., 3 g fiber, 30 g pro.

Sweet onions serve as vessels for a savory mixture of farro, turkey sausage, feta cheese, and carrots. A crisp green salad makes a nice accompaniment.

stuffed onions

PREP: 20 minutes **SLOW COOK:** 3½ hours (low) or 2½ hours (high)

¾   **cup cooked farro**
½   **cup cooked and crumbled turkey sausage**
½   **cup crumbled feta cheese**
¼   **cup finely chopped carrot**
¼   **teaspoon Italian seasoning**
¼   **teaspoon salt**
4   **medium sweet onions (about 2½ pounds)**
1   **cup chicken broth**
¼   **cup snipped fresh basil**

1. In a large bowl combine the cooked farro, cooked turkey sausage, ¼ cup of the feta cheese, carrot, Italian seasoning, and salt. Set aside.

2. Peel and cut a thin slice from the end of each onion. Using a spoon or a melon baller, scoop out the inside of each onion, leaving a ¼- to ½-inch shell. Stuff the onions with the turkey mixture, mounding as needed.

3. Pour the chicken broth in a 4- to 6-quart oval slow cooker. Place the stuffed onions in the cooker; make sure each onion is sitting flat on the bottom of the cooker.

4. Cover and cook on low-heat setting for 3½ to 4 hours or on high-heat setting for 2½ to 3 hours. To serve, cut each onion in half. Top the onion halves with the remaining feta cheese and basil. **Makes 4 servings.**

PER SERVING: 256 cal., 7 g fat (4 g sat. fat), 43 mg chol., 706 mg sodium, 33 g carb., 5 g fiber, 15 g pro.

cook smart Don't let the farro make you shy away from this recipe. It's a whole grain that is related to wheat and can be found in the health or bulk food section of many supermarkets. It boasts 5 grams fiber per ¼ cup. If you can't find it, use wheat berries or cooked barley instead.

Choose the chutney you use in this sweetly aromatic dish based on how hot you like your food.

mango chutney chicken

PREP: 20 minutes   **SLOW COOK:** 5 hours (low) or 2½ hours (high)

1	medium onion, cut into wedges
8	bone-in chicken thighs, skinned (about 3 pounds)
6	medium carrots, peeled and cut into 1-inch pieces (about 3 cups)
⅛	teaspoon salt
⅛	teaspoon ground black pepper
½	cup mango chutney
½	cup low-calorie barbecue sauce
⅓	cup golden raisins
¼	cup currants
1	teaspoon curry powder
2⅔	cups hot cooked brown rice
¼	cup toasted cashews, coarsely chopped
2	tablespoons thinly sliced green onion (1)

1. Place onion wedges in a 3½- or 4-quart slow cooker. Remove any visible fat from chicken. Place chicken and carrots in cooker; sprinkle with salt and pepper. Snip any large pieces of chutney. In a small bowl combine barbecue sauce, chutney, golden raisins, currants, and curry powder; pour over chicken.

2. Cover and cook on low-heat setting for 5 to 5½ hours or on high-heat setting for 2½ to 2¾ hours. Remove chicken from cooker. Stir onion and sauce in cooker.

3. Serve onion and sauce over chicken and rice. Top with cashews and green onion slices. **Makes 8 servings.**

PER SERVING: 354 cal., 7 g fat (2 g sat. fat), 97 mg chol., 513 mg sodium, 50 g carb., 4 g fiber, 23 g pro.

cook smart Chicken thigh meat gets super tender and moist when cooked in a slow cooker. Skinning chicken thighs makes them much lower in fat and calories, so you can enjoy this succulent meat even when you're watching your weight. You'll save about 4 grams fat and 45 calories by removing the skin from each chicken thigh.

This recipe easily re-creates a takeout favorite at home that's far more healthful than the original.

asian chicken lettuce wraps

PREP: 25 minutes   **SLOW COOK:** 4 hours (low) or 2 hours (high)

Nonstick cooking spray
2   pounds uncooked ground chicken breast
3   green onions
1   8-ounce can water chestnuts, drained and chopped
1   cup shredded carrots (2 medium)
1   cup frozen sweet soybeans (edamame)
4   teaspoons reduced-sodium soy sauce
1   tablespoon Chinese-style hot mustard
2   teaspoons reduced-sodium teriyaki sauce
1   teaspoon rice vinegar
½   teaspoon ground black pepper
1   14.5-ounce can reduced-sodium chicken broth
2   tablespoons hoisin sauce
12 leaves butterhead (Bibb or Boston) lettuce or iceberg lettuce
    Asian chili sauce (optional)
    Sesame seeds (optional)

1. Lightly coat a large skillet with cooking spray. Heat skillet over medium-high heat. Add chicken to skillet and cook until no longer pink, using a wooden spoon to break up meat as it cooks. Thinly slice white parts of green onions; set aside. Cut the green parts of green onions into slivers; set aside.

2. In a 3½- or 4-quart slow cooker combine cooked chicken, the white parts of green onions, the water chestnuts, carrots, frozen edamame, soy sauce, mustard, teriyaki sauce, vinegar, and pepper. Pour chicken broth over all.

3. Cover and cook on low-heat setting for 4 to 5 hours or on high-heat setting for 2 to 2½ hours.

4. Strain mixture, discarding cooking liquid. Stir hoisin sauce and the green onion slivers into chicken mixture. Serve with lettuce leaves and, if desired, Asian chili sauce and sesame seeds. **Makes 6 servings.**

PER SERVING: 258 cal., 4 g fat (1 g sat. fat), 88 mg chol., 538 mg sodium, 13 g carb., 3 g fiber, 40 g pro.

cook smart Edamame is a green soybean harvested when the beans are still green and sweet tasting. A ½-cup portion of shelled edamame has 13 grams of soy protein and 5 grams of fiber, both of which can help prevent heart disease. Look for them either frozen or in the produce section of your grocery store.

● LOW CALORIE

The veggies are "roasted" in the slow cooker, so your house stays cool—and you can do other things as they cook. The veggies and the chicken-apple sausages give these sandwiches great flavor.

sausage sandwiches with roasted veggies

PREP: 10 minutes   **SLOW COOK:** 6½ hours (low) or 3 hours (high)

Nonstick cooking spray
2 teaspoons olive oil
2 chicken-apple sausage links or two 4-inch pieces smoked turkey sausage
1 medium green sweet pepper, sliced
1 medium onion, cut into 12 wedges
1 cup grape tomatoes
4 cloves garlic, minced
1 teaspoon dried oregano, crushed
3 tablespoons light mayonnaise or salad dressing
1½ teaspoons packed dark brown sugar
1½ teaspoons mustard
4 whole wheat hot dog buns, lightly toasted

1. Coat a 3½- or 4-quart slow cooker with cooking spray. In a medium nonstick skillet heat 1 teaspoon of the oil over medium heat; add sausage. Cook until brown on all sides, turning links frequently.

2. Add the remaining 1 teaspoon oil, the sweet pepper, onion, tomatoes, garlic, and oregano to slow cooker, tossing until combined. Arrange sausages on top of mixture in cooker.

3. Cover and cook on low-heat setting for 6½ to 7 hours or on high-heat setting for 3 to 3½ hours.

4. Meanwhile, for sauce, in a small bowl whisk together mayonnaise, brown sugar, and mustard; cover with plastic wrap. Chill until serving time.

5. To serve, spoon about ⅓ cup of the vegetable mixture into each bun. Cut each sausage piece in half lengthwise; place each half, cut side down, on top of vegetables. Spoon the sauce over sausage. **Makes 4 servings.**

PER SERVING: 259 cal., 10 g fat (2 g sat. fat), 16 mg chol., 481 mg sodium, 34 g carb., 3 g fiber, 8 g pro.

● HIGH FIBER   ● GLUTEN FREE

To serve this dish, first scoop out the shrimp and spinach from the top of the polenta. Ladle the polenta into serving bowls, then top with the shrimp, spinach, tomatoes, avocado, and cilantro.

mexican shrimp polenta

PREP: 15 minutes   **SLOW COOK:** 3½ hours (high)

	Nonstick cooking spray
3½	cups water
2	cups frozen whole kernel corn, thawed
1½	cups shredded cheddar cheese
1¼	cups polenta-style cornmeal
2	4-ounce cans diced green chiles
½	cup fat-free milk
½	teaspoon ground ancho chile pepper
¼	teaspoon salt
⅛	teaspoon ground black pepper
1½	pounds fresh peeled, deveined medium shrimp
4	cups fresh baby spinach
2	cups cherry tomatoes, halved
2	medium avocados, halved, seeded, peeled, and chopped
¼	cup fresh cilantro leaves

1. Coat a 4-quart slow cooker with cooking spray. Add the water, corn, cheese, cornmeal, chiles, and milk to the slow cooker. Whisk to combine. Cover and cook on high-heat setting for 3 to 4 hours, stirring every hour throughout cooking.

2. In a medium bowl combine ancho chile pepper, salt, and pepper. Add shrimp and toss to coat. Layer shrimp and spinach on top of polenta. Cover and cook 30 to 45 minutes more or until shrimp are opaque.

3. To serve, ladle polenta, then shrimp and spinach, into serving bowls. Sprinkle with tomatoes, avocados, and cilantro. **Makes 8 servings.**

PER SERVING: 370 cal., 15 g fat (6 g sat. fat), 152 mg chol., 436 mg sodium, 34 g carb., 5 g fiber, 28 g pro.

sides

Keep the main dish simple—such as roasted or grilled meat—and
round out the meal with a special, fuss-free side (or two).

Sweet and savory at the same time, this squash side pairs well with roasted pork.

acorn squash with rustic raisin sauce

PREP: 20 minutes   **SLOW COOK:** 4 hours (low) or 2 hours (high)

Nonstick cooking spray
1½ pounds acorn squash (1 large)
⅛ teaspoon salt
½ cup chopped onion (1 medium)
⅓ cup raisins
2 tablespoons water
1 teaspoon apple pie spice
2 tablespoons lower-fat margarine
4 teaspoons honey
1 teaspoon vanilla
2 tablespoons chopped pistachio
    nuts or slivered almonds

1. Lightly coat a 3½- or 4-quart slow cooker with cooking spray; set aside.

2. Cut squash into four wedges, discarding stem, seeds, and strings. Sprinkle cut sides of squash with salt. Set aside. In the prepared slow cooker combine onion, raisins, the water, and apple pie spice. Place squash wedges, cut sides down, on top of onion mixture, making sure that an edge of each squash wedge touches the onion mixture.

3. Cover and cook on low-heat setting for 4 to 5 hours or on high-heat setting for 2 to 2½ hours.

4. Place the squash wedges, cut sides up, on serving plates. Stir margarine, honey, and vanilla into onion mixture in slow cooker. Spoon onion mixture over squash wedges. Sprinkle with pistachio nuts. **Makes 4 servings.**

PER SERVING: 169 cal., 5 g fat (1 g sat. fat), 0 mg chol., 149 mg sodium, 32 g carb., 3 g fiber, 3 g pro.

Smoked paprika comes in both sweet and hot varieties. Either one works here. What you use depends on what you like or what you have in your spice cupboard.

spicy mashed sweet potatoes

PREP: 20 minutes   **SLOW COOK:** 6 hours (low) or 3 hours (high)

Nonstick cooking spray
2½   pounds sweet potatoes, peeled and cubed
⅓   cup chopped red onion (1 small)
1   4-ounce can diced green chiles
3   cloves garlic, minced
1   teaspoon ground cumin
½   teaspoon salt
½   teaspoon smoked paprika
½   cup reduced-sodium chicken broth
1   tablespoon snipped fresh cilantro

1. Lightly coat the inside of a 3½- or 4-quart slow cooker with nonstick spray. Add sweet potatoes, red onion, diced green chiles, garlic, cumin, salt, and smoked paprika. Pour broth over all.

2. Cover and cook on low-heat setting for 6 to 7 hours or on high-heat setting for 3 to 3½ hours or until very tender. Mash with a potato masher. Garnish with cilantro. **Makes 10 servings.**

PER SERVING: 78 cal., 0 g fat, 0 mg chol., 221 mg sodium, 18 g carb., 3 g fiber, 2 g pro.

cook smart It's no secret that sweet potatoes are more nutritious than white potatoes, but do you know why? Per half cup, sweet potatoes provide 3 grams more fiber, five times more iron, seven times more calcium, four times more vitamin C, and exponentially more vitamin A. The extra calories and carbohydrates in sweet potatoes are worth the splurge for all those nutrients.

Serve these creamy, cheesy potatoes with grilled lean steak or roasted chicken.

blue cheese and onion yukon golds

PREP: 10 minutes   **SLOW COOK:** 5½ hours (low) or 2¾ hours (high)

Nonstick cooking spray
2   **medium onions, thinly sliced**
½   **cup reduced-sodium chicken broth**
1   **teaspoon garlic, minced**
4   **6-ounce Yukon gold potatoes, cut in half lengthwise**
¼   **teaspoon salt**
⅛   **to ¼ teaspoon ground black pepper**
1   **ounce crumbled reduced-fat blue cheese**

1. Coat a 3½- or 4-quart slow cooker with cooking spray. In cooker combine onions, broth, and garlic, tossing until well coated. Place potatoes on top of onion mixture.

2. Cover and cook on low-heat setting for 5½ to 6 hours or on high-heat setting for 2¾ to 3 hours.

3. Remove potatoes; fluff each half with a fork.

4. Stir salt and pepper into onion mixture in cooker. Divide onion mixture among potato halves. Sprinkle evenly with cheese. **Makes 4 servings.**

PER SERVING: 177 cal., 1 g fat (1 g sat. fat), 4 mg chol., 323 mg sodium, 35 g carb., 5 g fiber, 6 g pro.

These sweet and earthy root vegetables get a burst of brightness from pomegranate juice. Serve alongside roasted meat or chilled on top of baby spinach leaves.

sweet ginger roots

PREP: 15 minutes   **SLOW COOK:** 6½ hours (low) or 3¼ hours (high)

¾	cup pomegranate juice
1	tablespoon cornstarch
¼	teaspoon salt
¼	cup sugar
2	teaspoons grated fresh ginger
2¾	pounds red and/or golden beets, trimmed, peeled, and cut into ¾-inch wedges* (6 medium)
12	ounces carrots, peeled and cut into 3-inch pieces (halve any thick pieces) (4 medium)

1. In a medium saucepan whisk together pomegranate juice, cornstarch, and salt until cornstarch is dissolved. Bring to boiling over medium-high heat; continue boiling for 1 minute. Stir in the sugar; cool completely. Stir in ginger.

2. In a 3½- or 4-quart slow cooker combine the pomegranate juice mixture, beets, and carrots.

3. Cover and cook on low-heat setting for 6½ to 7 hours or on high-heat setting for 3¼ to 3½ hours. Stir to coat vegetables.

4. Serve warm as a side dish or chilled as a salad. **Makes 8 servings.**

*****Tip:** To peel beets easily, use a vegetable peeler and peel the beets under slow running water. The water prevents the beets from staining your fingertips.

PER SERVING: 126 cal., 0 g fat, 0 mg chol., 226 mg sodium, 29 g carb., 6 g fiber, 3 g pro.

This warm and creamy potato salad is an excellent complement to grilled chicken or fish, lean steak, or even fried eggs.

green beans and petite reds

PREP: 20 minutes **SLOW COOK:** 4 hours (low) or 2 hours (high)

Nonstick cooking spray

1 pound fresh green beans, trimmed

1 pound tiny new potatoes, quartered

1 cup chopped onion (1 large)

¼ cup water

¼ teaspoon salt

¼ teaspoon ground black pepper

¼ cup light mayonnaise or salad dressing

¼ cup fat-free sour cream

1 to 2 tablespoons fat-free milk

1 tablespoon Dijon mustard

1 tablespoon lemon juice

½ teaspoon dried tarragon, crushed

¼ teaspoon salt

Ground black pepper

1. Coat a 3½- or 4-quart slow cooker with cooking spray. In the prepared cooker combine beans, potatoes, onion, potatoes, the water, ¼ teaspoon salt, and pepper.

2. Cover and cook on low-heat setting for 4 hours or on high-heat setting for 2 hours.

3. Meanwhile, for sauce, in a small bowl whisk together mayonnaise, sour cream, milk, mustard, lemon juice, tarragon, and ¼ teaspoon salt. Cover with plastic wrap and chill until needed.

4. To serve, stir the sauce into mixture in cooker, tossing until vegetables are coated. Sprinkle with additional pepper. **Makes 8 servings.**

PER SERVING: 100 cal., 3 g fat (0 g sat. fat), 3 mg chol., 270 mg sodium, 17 g carb., 3 g fiber, 3 g pro.

This recipe makes enough for a crowd, so consider serving it for company. Alternatively, enjoy a larger portion for a vegetarian, fiber-rich main-dish meal.

wild rice with corn and basil

PREP: 25 minutes   **SLOW COOK:** 4 hours (low) or 2½ hours (high)

2	teaspoons vegetable oil
1½	cups chopped onions (3 medium)
2	cloves garlic, minced
	Nonstick cooking spray
2½	cups chopped yellow, orange, and/or red sweet peppers (2 large)
¾	cup uncooked wild rice, rinsed and drained
¾	cup frozen whole kernel corn
½	teaspoon salt
2¼	cups boiling water
¾	cup chopped pecans, toasted (see tip, page 23)
⅓	cup snipped fresh basil

1. In a large skillet heat oil over medium heat. Add onions and garlic; cook and stir just until onions are tender.

2. Lightly coat a 3- or 3½-quart slow cooker with cooking spray. Add onion mixture, sweet peppers, uncooked rice, frozen corn, and salt; stir in the boiling water.

3. Cover and cook on low-heat setting for 4 hours or on high-heat setting for 2½ hours.

4. To serve, stir in pecans and basil. **Makes 12 servings.**

PER SERVING: 119 cal., 6 g fat (1 g sat. fat), 0 mg chol., 101 mg sodium, 15 g carb., 2 g fiber, 3 g pro.

cook smart Wild rice is actually a grass that is native to the United States. While it looks like rice, the flavor is nuttier and the texture has a toothy bite. The long cook time makes it ideal for the slow cooker. As a bonus, wild rice has more protein and fewer calories and carbohydrates compared with brown rice.

Creamy and wholesome, this so-simple risotto skips stirring in favor of slow cooking.

spinach-basil brown rice risotto

PREP: 20 minutes   **SLOW COOK:** 4 hours (low) or 2 hours (high)

Nonstick cooking spray
1½ cups uncooked brown rice
1 cup chopped red or green sweet pepper
¾ teaspoon salt
3½ cups water
2 cups packed fresh spinach, coarsely chopped (2 ounces)
¼ to ½ cup snipped fresh basil
¼ cup pine nuts or slivered almonds, toasted (see tip, page 23)
2 tablespoons olive oil
1 teaspoon grated lemon peel
1 clove garlic, minced
Grated Parmesan cheese (optional)

1. Coat a 4-quart slow cooker with cooking spray. In the prepared cooker combine uncooked rice, sweet pepper, and salt. Pour the water over mixture in cooker.

2. Cover and cook on low-heat setting for 4 to 5 hours or on high-heat setting for 2 to 2½ hours or until rice is tender.

3. Stir spinach, basil, pine nuts, oil, lemon peel, and garlic into mixture in cooker until spinach is wilted. If desired, top with cheese. **Makes 10 servings.**

PER SERVING: 156 cal., 6 g fat (1 g sat. fat), 0 mg chol., 184 mg sodium, 23 g carb., 2 g fiber, 3 g pro.

Toothsome pearls of pasta are tossed with loads of veggies in this colorful dish. Try it with roasted or grilled chicken or fish.

italian vegetable couscous

PREP: 25 minutes   **SLOW COOK:** 7 hours (low) or 3½ hours (high) + 20 minutes (high)

2   14½-ounce cans diced tomatoes, drained

1   15-ounce can cannellini beans (white kidney beans), rinsed and drained

1   14½-ounce can reduced-sodium chicken broth

2   tablespoons red wine vinegar

1   medium zucchini, halved lengthwise and sliced (1¼ cups)

1   medium yellow summer squash, halved lengthwise and sliced (1¼ cups)

1   small red onion, cut into thin wedges

1   teaspoon snipped fresh rosemary

2   cloves garlic, minced

¼   teaspoon salt

¼   teaspoon ground black pepper

2   cups Israeli (large pearl) couscous (10 ounces)

2   tablespoons pine nuts, toasted (see tip, page 23)

1. In a 3½- or 4-quart slow cooker combine drained tomatoes, beans, chicken broth, red wine vinegar, zucchini, summer squash, onion, rosemary, garlic, salt, and pepper.

2. Cover and cook on low-heat setting for 7 to 8 hours or on high-heat setting for 3½ to 4 hours. If using low-heat setting, turn to high-heat setting. Stir in couscous. Cover and cook for 20 to 25 minutes more or until couscous is tender. Fluff with a fork. Garnish with pine nuts. **Makes 16 servings.**

PER SERVING: 114 cal., 1 g fat (0 g sat. fat), 0 mg chol., 243 mg sodium, 21 g carb., 3 g fiber, 5 g pro.

This salad tastes so fresh, you'd never dream it was prepared in a slow cooker. The zucchini and sweet pepper cook for just 20 minutes, so their texture stays crisp. Serve it warm or chilled.

wheat berry salad

PREP: 30 minutes   **SLOW COOK:** 8 hours (low) or 4 hours (high)

2	cups wheat berries
1	32-ounce carton reduced-sodium chicken broth
2	cups water
1	medium carrot, peeled and chopped
½	cup chopped onion (1 medium)
1½	teaspoons Italian seasoning, crushed
2	cloves garlic, minced
1	large zucchini, halved lengthwise and cut into ½-inch slices
1	medium red or yellow sweet pepper, cut into bite-size pieces
2	tablespoons lemon juice
2	tablespoons olive oil
2	teaspoons honey
2	cups grape or cherry tomatoes, halved
¼	teaspoon salt
⅛	teaspoon ground black pepper
½	cup crumbled ricotta salata or goat cheese (2 ounces)

1. Rinse and drain wheat berries. In a 3½- or 4-quart slow cooker combine wheat berries, chicken broth, the water, carrot, onion, Italian seasoning, and garlic.

2. Cover and cook on low-heat setting for 8 to 10 hours or on high-heat setting for 4 to 5 hours or until wheat berries and vegetables are tender, adding the zucchini and sweet pepper the last 20 minutes of cooking. Drain mixture.

3. In a screw-top jar combine lemon juice, olive oil, and honey. Cover and shake well. Pour over salad mixture. Add tomatoes and toss to combine. Season with salt and black pepper. Top with cheese. Serve warm or chill and serve cold. **Makes 16 servings.**

PER SERVING: 127 cal., 3 g fat (1 g sat. fat), 3 mg chol., 191 mg sodium, 20 g carb., 4 g fiber, 6 g pro.

When pulled pork is on the menu, cook up a batch of these flavorful, low-fat beans (just 2 grams per serving) flavored with a smoked turkey leg.

smoky beans

PREP: 15 minutes   **SLOW COOK:** 8 hours (low) or 4 hours (high)

1	smoked turkey drumstick (about 1 pound)
2	15-ounce cans navy or Great Northern beans, rinsed and drained
1	15-ounce can red beans or pinto beans, rinsed and drained
1	14½-ounce can diced tomatoes and green chiles
1	cup chicken broth
1	medium yellow or red sweet pepper, chopped
1	medium onion, chopped
2	tablespoons packed brown sugar
3	cloves garlic, chopped
1	teaspoon dry mustard
½	teaspoon dried savory or thyme, crushed

1. In a 5 to 6-quart slow cooker combine the smoked turkey drumstick, beans, diced tomatoes and green chiles, broth, sweet pepper, onion, brown sugar, garlic, dry mustard, and savory.

2. Cover and cook on low-heat setting for 8 to 10 hours or on high-heat setting for 4 to 5 hours. Remove turkey drumstick. When cool enough to handle, remove meat from bone and coarsely chop. Discard skin and bone. Return meat to bean mixture. **Makes 14 servings.**

PER SERVING: 137 cal., 2 g fat (1 g sat. fat), 32 mg chol., 492 mg sodium, 21 g carb., 5 g fiber, 13 g pro.

desserts

Satisfy your sweet tooth with lightened-up treats such as cheesecake, bread pudding, hot chocolate, and brownies.

You can make a divine cheesecake that's silky, creamy, and low in calories in your slow cooker. This refreshing orange version takes the work out of a complicated dessert.

ginger-orange cheesecake

PREP: 25 minutes   **SLOW COOK:** 2½ hours (high)   **CHILL:** 4 hours

Nonstick cooking spray
12 ounces reduced-fat cream cheese (Neufchâtel), softened
½ cup sugar
2 tablespoons orange juice
1 tablespoon all-purpose flour
½ teaspoon vanilla
½ cup nonfat sour cream
¾ cup refrigerated or frozen egg product, thawed, or 3 eggs, lightly beaten
1 cup warm water
2 medium Cara Cara and/or blood oranges, sliced
1 teaspoon finely shredded orange peel
Finely chopped crystallized ginger (optional)

1. Lightly coat a 1½-quart soufflé dish or casserole* with cooking spray. Tear off an 18×12-inch piece of heavy foil; cut in half lengthwise. Fold each piece lengthwise into thirds. Crisscross the foil strips and place the dish in the center of the crisscross; set aside.

2. For filling, in a large bowl beat cream cheese, sugar, orange juice, flour, and vanilla with an electric mixer on medium speed until combined. Beat in sour cream until smooth. Beat in eggs with mixer on low speed just until combined. Stir in orange peel. Pour filling into prepared dish. Cover dish tightly with foil.

3. Pour the warm water into a 3½- to 5-quart slow cooker. Using the ends of the foil strips, transfer dish to cooker. Leave foil strips under dish.

4. Cover and cook on high-heat setting for 2½ hours or until center is set. Using foil strips, carefully remove dish from cooker; discard foil strips. Cool completely, uncovered, on a wire rack. Cover and chill for 4 to 24 hours before serving.

5. Garnish with orange slices and, if desired, crystallized ginger. **Makes 10 servings.**

***Tip:** Before beginning this recipe, check to make sure that the dish or casserole you plan to use fits into your slow cooker.

PER SERVING: 161 cal., 8 g fat (4 g sat. fat), 26 mg chol., 159 mg sodium, 17 g carb., 1 g fiber, 6 g pro.

cook smart If you've never tried a Cara Cara orange, it's worth seeking them out. They are a variety of navel orange that looks similar on the outside but has a pink interior. They are nice and sweet, making them an excellent choice for a dessert recipe. Blood oranges, on the other hand, have a deep red wine-color interior with a more tart flavor. They are high in anthocyanins, antioxidants that can help protect against cancer. Both orange varieties are available from December through April.

Take the work out of making cobbler by letting your slow cooker do it for you. Choose a whole grain muffin mix to make this dessert even more healthful.

triple berry cobbler

PREP: 15 minutes   **SLOW COOK:** 3 hours (low) + 1 hour (high)   **COOL:** 30 minutes

Nonstick cooking spray
1   14-ounce package frozen loose-pack mixed berries
1   21-ounce can blueberry pie filling
2   tablespoons sugar
1   6½-ounce package blueberry muffin mix
⅓   cup water
2   tablespoons vegetable oil
    Plain Greek yogurt (optional)
    Honey (optional)

1. Lightly coat a 3½- or 4-quart slow cooker with cooking spray; set aside.

2. In cooker combine frozen berries, pie filling, and sugar.

3. Cover and cook on low-heat setting for 3 hours. Turn cooker to high-heat setting. In a medium bowl combine muffin mix, the water, and oil; stir just until combined. Spoon muffin mixture over berry mixture.

4. Cover and cook for 1 hour more or until a wooden toothpick inserted into center of muffin mixture comes out clean. Turn off cooker. If possible, remove crockery liner from cooker. Cool, uncovered, for 30 to 45 minutes on a wire rack before serving.

5. If desired, serve with yogurt and honey. **Makes 12 servings.**

PER SERVING: 162 cal., 4 g fat (1 g sat. fat), 0 mg chol., 116 mg sodium, 31 g carb., 3 g fiber, 1 g pro.

Celebrate the perfect peaches of August with this fruited coffee cake. Leftovers make a special breakfast treat the next morning.

peach coffee cake with blackberries

PREP: 15 minutes   **SLOW COOK:** 2¼ hours (high)   **COOL:** 5 minutes

Disposable slow cooker liner
3   **medium peaches, peeled, pitted, and sliced, or 3 cups frozen unsweetened peach slices, thawed**
2   **cups fresh blackberries**
2   **teaspoons grated fresh ginger**
2   **cups all-purpose flour**
1   **teaspoon baking soda**
1   **teaspoon ground cinnamon**
½   **teaspoon baking powder**
¼   **teaspoon salt**
⅓   **cup butter, softened**
½   **cup packed brown sugar**
½   **cup frozen or refrigerated egg product, or 2 eggs**
1   **tablespoon vanilla**
1   **cup fat-free Greek yogurt**
    Powdered sugar or frozen light whipped dessert topping, thawed (optional)

1. Line a 3½- or 4-quart slow cooker with a slow cooker liner. Add peaches, blackberries, and ginger and toss to coat.

2. In a medium bowl combine flour, baking soda, cinnamon, baking powder, and salt.

3. In a large mixing bowl beat butter with an electric mixer on medium to high speed for 30 seconds. Beat in brown sugar until combined. Beat in eggs and vanilla. Beat in half of the flour mixture. Beat in the yogurt. Beat in remaining flour mixture until combined. Spread over fruit.

4. Place a clean kitchen towel over top of slow cooker, then top cooker with lid. Cook on high-heat setting for 2¼ to 2½ hours or until a toothpick inserted in center of the cake layer comes out clean. If possible, carefully rotate crockery liner halfway through cooking time to ensure even cooking.

5. Remove crockery liner from cooker, if possible, or turn off cooker. Cool on a wire rack for 5 minutes. Remove lid and towel. To unmold cake, place a large plate over the crockery liner. Using pot holders, carefully invert crockery liner onto plate (do not lift by the edges of the disposable liner). Remove the disposable liner. Serve cake warm or at room temperature. If desired, dust with powdered sugar or serve with light whipped dessert topping. **Makes 10 servings.**

PER SERVING: 241 cal., 7 g fat (4 g sat. fat), 0 mg chol., 298 mg sodium, 39 g carb., 3 g fiber, 7 g pro.

Some slow cookers may be hotter on one side, so rotate this delicate clafouti-like dessert halfway through cooking for even browning.

lemon-berry pudding cake

STAND: 30 minutes   **PREP:** 20 minutes   **SLOW COOK:** 2½ hours (high)   **COOL:** 1 hour

3   eggs
     Nonstick cooking spray
1   cup fresh blueberries and/or fresh
     red raspberries
1   tablespoon granulated sugar
½   cup granulated sugar
¼   cup all-purpose flour
2   teaspoons finely shredded lemon
     peel
¼   teaspoon salt
1   cup fat-free milk
3   tablespoons lemon juice
3   tablespoons tub-style vegetable
     oil spread
     Powdered sugar (optional)

1. Let eggs stand at room temperature for 30 minutes. Meanwhile, coat a 2-quart slow cooker with cooking spray. Place berries in cooker and sprinkle with the 1 tablespoon granulated sugar.

2. For batter, separate eggs. In a medium bowl combine the ½ cup granulated sugar, the flour, lemon peel, and salt. Add milk, lemon juice, vegetable oil spread, and egg yolks. Beat with an electric mixer on low speed until combined. Beat on medium speed for 1 minute.

3. Thoroughly wash beaters. In another bowl beat egg whites with an electric mixer on medium speed until soft peaks form (tips curl). Fold egg whites into batter. Carefully pour batter over berries in cooker, spreading evenly.

4. Cover and cook on high-heat setting for 2½ to 3 hours. If cake begins to look too brown on one side, rotate the crockery liner 180° halfway through cooking. Turn off cooker. If possible, remove crockery liner from cooker; cool, uncovered, for 1 hour on a wire rack before serving.

5. If desired, sprinkle with powdered sugar. **Makes 6 servings.**

PER SERVING: 200 cal., 7 g fat (2 g sat. fat), 107 mg chol., 187 mg sodium, 29 g carb., 1 g fiber, 5 g pro.

Start the slow cooker in late afternoon, and after your dinner has settled and you're craving something sweet, this warm and comforting rice pudding will be ready and waiting.

rice pudding with apricots and a cherry swirl

PREP: 20 minutes   **SLOW COOK:** 4½ hours (low)

	Nonstick cooking spray
6½	cups water
1⅓	cups converted rice (do not substitute long grain rice)
½	cup sugar
1	cup snipped dried apricots and/or dried cherries
2	tablespoons butter, softened
1	tablespoon vanilla
¾	teaspoon ground cardamom
1	6-ounce container vanilla Greek yogurt
½	cup cherry preserves

1. Coat a 3½- or 4-quart slow cooker with cooking spray; set aside. In a large bowl combine the water, uncooked rice, and sugar. Add apricots, butter, vanilla, and cardamom. Stir well to combine. Transfer to prepared slow cooker.

2. Cover and cook on low-heat setting for 4½ hours (do not stir). Turn off heat; stir in yogurt. Serve warm.

3. Just before serving, in a small saucepan heat cherry preserves until melted (or place in a small microwave-safe bowl and microwave on 100-percent power [high] for 30 seconds).

4. Stir rice pudding before serving. Top each serving with 1 to 2 teaspoons cherry preserves. **Makes 16 servings.**

PER SERVING: 152 cal., 1 g fat (1 g sat. fat), 4 mg chol., 23 mg sodium, 32 g carb., 1 g fiber, 2 g pro.

Swap vanilla extract for the almond extract if you like—or use raisins instead of dried cherries.

chocolate-cherry bread pudding

PREP: 25 minutes   **SLOW COOK:** 3 hours (low)   **COOL:** 30 minutes

Nonstick cooking spray
½   cup refrigerated or frozen egg product, thawed, or 2 eggs, lightly beaten
¼   cup sugar
¼   teaspoon almond extract
⅛   teaspoon salt
1   cup fat-free milk
3   cups dried whole wheat bread cubes*
½   cup chopped bittersweet chocolate (2 ounces)
⅓   cup dried tart cherries
1   cup warm water
3   tablespoons powdered sugar
2   tablespoons low-fat Greek yogurt
1   teaspoon fat-free milk
3   tablespoons sliced almonds, toasted (see tip, page 23) (optional)

1. Lightly coat a 1-quart soufflé dish or casserole** with cooking spray. Tear off an 18×12-inch piece of heavy foil; cut in half lengthwise. Fold each piece lengthwise into thirds. Crisscross the foil strips and place the dish in the center of the crisscross; set aside.

2. In a medium bowl combine eggs, sugar, almond extract, and salt. Whisk in the 1 cup milk. Gently stir in bread cubes, chocolate, and cherries. Pour mixture into prepared dish. Cover dish tightly with foil.

3. Pour the warm water into a 3½- to 5-quart slow cooker. Using the ends of the foil strips, transfer dish to cooker. Leave foil strips under dish.

4. Cover and cook on low-heat setting for 3 to 3½ hours or until a knife inserted in center comes out clean. Using foil strips, carefully remove dish from cooker; discard foil strips. Cool, uncovered, on a wire rack for 30 minutes before serving.

5. Meanwhile, for icing, in a small bowl combine powdered sugar, yogurt, and the 1 teaspoon milk. Drizzle cooled bread pudding with icing. If desired, sprinkle with almonds. **Makes 6 servings.**

*****Tip:** To make dry bread cubes, preheat oven to 300°F. Cut whole wheat bread slices (about 3 ounces) into cubes to make 3 cups. Spread cubes in a single layer in a 15×10×1-inch baking pan. Bake for 10 to 15 minutes or until dry, stirring twice; cool.

******Tip:** Before beginning this recipe, check to make sure that the dish or casserole you plan to use fits into your slow cooker.

PER SERVING: 189 cal., 4 g fat (2 g sat. fat), 1 mg chol., 178 mg sodium, 34 g carb., 2 g fiber, 6 g pro.

cook smart The U.S. Food and Drug Administration doesn't have a firm definition for bittersweet chocolate, just that it must contain a certain amount of cacao. Among chocolate manufacturers, there can be a wide range of cacao percentages in what is labeled as bittersweet chocolate. As the percentage increases, so does the intensity of flavor and the health benefits, which include the ability to lower blood pressure. For best results in baking, use a bittersweet chocolate that is about 60 percent cacao.

Brown sugar brings depth to the sweetness in this fruity compote. Serve it topped with low-fat vanilla ice cream or frozen yogurt for an irresistible hot-cold effect.

fruit compote with ginger

PREP: 15 minutes **SLOW COOK:** 6 hours (low) or 3 hours (high)

3   medium ripe yet firm fresh pears
1   15.5-ounce can pineapple chunks, undrained
1   cup dried apricots, quartered
3   tablespoons frozen orange juice concentrate
2   tablespoons packed brown sugar
1   tablespoon quick-cooking tapioca
1   teaspoon grated fresh ginger or ½ teaspoon ground ginger
2   cups frozen unsweetened pitted dark sweet cherries
    Flaked coconut, toasted (see tip, page 23)
    Macadamia nuts or pecans, chopped and toasted (see tip, page 23)

1. If desired, peel pears. Cut pears into quarters and remove cores. Cut pear quarters into chunks. In a 3½- or 4-quart slow cooker combine pears, pineapple, apricots, orange juice concentrate, brown sugar, tapioca, and ginger.

2. Cover and cook on low-heat setting for 6 to 8 hours or on high-heat setting for 3 to 4 hours. Stir in cherries.

3. Serve warm. Top each serving with coconut and nuts. **Makes 10 servings.**

PER SERVING: 128 cal., 0 g fat, 0 mg chol., 3 mg sodium, 33 g carb., 3 g fiber, 1 g pro.

cook smart Not only does fruit provide a low-calorie, low-fat sweet finish to a meal, including fruit as a dessert can help boost your overall fruit intake. It's a double bonus!

A mix of apples—tart Granny Smith combined with sweeter varieties—enhances the flavor of this warm apple dessert topped with a light vanilla custard.

apple confit

PREP: 30 minutes   **SLOW COOK:** 3 hours (low) or 1½ hours (high)

1½ pounds Granny Smith apples, peeled, cored, and thinly sliced (about ¼ inch thick)

1½ pounds McIntosh, Pippin, or Braeburn apples, peeled, cored, and thinly sliced (about ¼ inch thick)

¼ cup sugar

½ teaspoon ground cinnamon

1½ teaspoons vanilla

½ cup fat-free milk

2 tablespoons sugar

1 egg
Freshly grated nutmeg (optional)

2 tablespoons chopped toasted hazelnuts (see tip, page 23)

1. In a very large bowl combine sliced apples, ¼ cup sugar, and the cinnamon. Toss to coat. Place apple mixture in a 4- to 5-quart slow cooker.

2. Cover and cook on low-heat setting for 3 hours or on high-heat setting for 1½ hours or until tender but not turning to sauce. Stir in 1 teaspoon of the vanilla. Spoon into eight (6-ounce) ramekins or dessert dishes; set aside.

3. For crème anglaise, in a small saucepan heat milk until tiny bubbles form at the edge (do not boil). In a small bowl whisk together 2 tablespoons sugar and the egg. Gradually beat the warm milk into the egg mixture. Return mixture to the saucepan. Cook over medium heat for 2 to 4 minutes or until the mixture coats the back of a metal spoon, stirring constantly. Stir in remaining ½ teaspoon vanilla.

4. To serve, spoon crème anglaise over warm apple confit. If desired, sprinkle crème anglaise with grated nutmeg. Sprinkle with hazelnuts. **Makes 8 servings.**

PER SERVING: 144 cal., 2 g fat (0 g sat. fat), 24 mg chol., 17 mg sodium, 32 g carb., 4 g fiber, 2 g pro.

This is the classic baked apple dessert, only made in a slow cooker. Play around with the spices and dried fruit options until you find your favorite mix.

stuffed apples

PREP: 20 minutes   **SLOW COOK:** 5 hours (low) or 2½ hours (high)

4   medium tart baking apples (such as Granny Smith)
⅓   cup snipped dried figs or raisins
¼   cup packed brown sugar
½   teaspoon apple pie spice or ground cinnamon
¼   cup apple juice
1   tablespoon butter or margarine, cut into 4 pieces

1. Core apples; cut a strip of peel from the top of each apple. Place apples, top sides up, in a 3½- or 4-quart slow cooker.

2. In a small bowl combine figs, brown sugar, and apple pie spice. Spoon mixture into centers of apples, patting in with a knife or narrow metal spatula. Pour apple juice around apples in cooker. Top each apple with a piece of butter.

3. Cover and cook on low-heat setting for 5 hours or on high-heat setting for 2½ hours.

4. Using a large spoon, transfer apples to dessert dishes. Spoon some of the cooking liquid over apples. Serve warm. **Makes 4 servings.**

PER SERVING: 200 cal., 3 g fat (2 g sat. fat), 8 mg chol., 31 mg sodium, 45 g carb., 5 g fiber, 1 g pro.

cook smart It's said that an apple a day keeps the doctor away, and that doesn't mean it can't be for dessert. With all the health benefits of apples, it's easy to believe. They are high in soluble fiber, which can help control cholesterol. They're also high in quercetin, which helps prevent Alzheimer's and Parkinson's diseases—and they can help protect against cancer as well. For even more bang for your nutrition buck, leave the peel on.

Tender, juicy pears get a just-sweet-enough sauce of chocolate, coconut milk, and coffee. Use your favorite pear variety and, if desired, decaffeinated coffee.

coconut-mocha poached pears

PREP: 20 minutes   **SLOW COOK:** 3½ hours (low)

6   medium ripe yet firm fresh pears
¼   cup sugar
2   tablespoons unsweetened cocoa powder
⅔   cup unsweetened light coconut milk
⅓   cup strong coffee
2   tablespoons coffee liqueur or strong coffee
    Light frozen whipped dessert topping, thawed (optional)
    Toasted coconut (see tip, page 23) (optional)
    Grated chocolate (optional)

1. Peel pears; quarter pears lengthwise and remove cores. Place pears in a 3½- or 4-quart slow cooker. In a bowl stir together sugar and cocoa powder. Stir in coconut milk, coffee, and liqueur. Pour mixture over pears in cooker.

2. Cover and cook on low-heat setting for 3½ to 4 hours or until pears are tender.

3. Using a slotted spoon, transfer pears to dessert dishes. Spoon cooking liquid over pears. If desired, top with dessert topping and sprinkle with coconut and chocolate. **Makes 8 servings.**

PER SERVING: 125 cal., 1 g fat (1 g sat. fat), 0 mg chol., 7 mg sodium, 29 g carb., 4 g fiber, 1 g pro.

This fruit dessert is a delightful combination of textures. The richness of the sweetened cream cheese enhances the tender poached pears—while the pistachios and candied ginger add a nice crunch.

poached pears with honeyed cream cheese

PREP: 15 minutes   **SLOW COOK:** 4 hours (low) or 2 hours (high)

8	small firm ripe pears, peeled, cored, and halved
½	teaspoon ground ginger
¼	teaspoon ground allspice
½	cup dry white wine
½	cup pear nectar or apple juice
½	cup reduced-fat cream cheese (Neufchâtel), softened
1	tablespoon honey
½	cup chopped pistachios
2	tablespoons finely chopped crystallized ginger

1. Place pears in a 3½- or 4-quart slow cooker. Sprinkle with ginger and allspice. Pour wine and pear nectar over pears.

2. Cover and cook on low-heat setting for 4 to 4½ hours or on high-heat setting for 2 to 2¼ hours.

3. In a small bowl combine cream cheese and honey. Use a slotted spoon to transfer pears to dessert dishes. Spoon cream cheese mixture into the hollows of the pears. Sprinkle with pistachios and crystallized ginger. Spoon some of the cooking liquid around the pears. **Makes 8 servings.**

PER SERVING: 183 cal., 7 g fat (2 g sat. fat), 10 mg chol., 51 mg sodium, 27 g carb., 4 g fiber, 3 g pro.

cook smart Dessert is often thought of as a guilt-producing course that you should avoid at all costs. This can lead to feelings of deprivation followed by caving into your cravings and going overboard later. A better approach is to occasionally indulge in your favorite treats, taking time to thoroughly enjoy every bite. With a little planning and reasonable portion sizes, an occasional splurge won't break your calorie budget.

This chocolaty dessert tastes like a cross between chocolate pudding, fudge, and a brownie—and with far fewer calories than you might expect.

fudgy brownies with strawberries

PREP: 15 minutes   **SLOW COOK:** 2½ hours (high)   **COOL:** 30 minutes

Nonstick cooking spray
- ¼ cup butter
- 2 ounces unsweetened chocolate
- ½ cup refrigerated or frozen egg product, thawed, or 2 eggs, lightly beaten
- ½ cup sugar
- ⅓ cup seedless sugar-free strawberry or red raspberry jam
- ¼ cup unsweetened applesauce
- 1 teaspoon vanilla
- ¾ cup all-purpose flour
- ¼ teaspoon baking powder
- ¼ teaspoon salt
- 1 cup warm water
- ¾ cup frozen light whipped dessert topping, thawed
- 3 cups sliced fresh strawberries or raspberries

1. Lightly coat a 1-quart soufflé dish or casserole* with cooking spray. Tear off an 18×12-inch piece of heavy foil; cut in half lengthwise. Fold each piece lengthwise into thirds. Crisscross the foil strips and place the dish in the center of the crisscross; set aside.

2. For batter, in a medium saucepan melt butter and chocolate over low heat. Remove from heat. Stir in eggs, sugar, jam, applesauce, and vanilla. Using a spoon, beat lightly until combined. Stir in flour, baking powder, and salt. Pour batter into prepared dish. Cover dish tightly with foil.

3. Pour the warm water into a 6-quart slow cooker. Using the ends of the foil strips, transfer dish to cooker. Leave foil strips under dish.

4. Cover and cook on high-heat setting for 2½ to 3 hours or until an internal temperature of 170°F registers on an instant-read thermometer. Using foil strips, carefully remove dish from cooker; discard foil strips. Turn off cooker. If possible, remove crockery liner from cooker. Cool for 30 minutes on a wire rack.

5. Top each serving with dessert topping and strawberries. **Makes 10 servings.**

***Tip:** Before beginning this recipe, check to make sure that the dish or casserole you plan to use fits into your slow cooker.

PER SERVING: 183 cal., 8 g fat (5 g sat. fat), 12 mg chol., 122 mg sodium, 27 g carb., 2 g fiber, 3 g pro.

cook smart Adding fresh fruit to an otherwise indulgent dessert bulks up the serving size, makes it take longer to eat, and ups the satisfaction factor. Plus, it makes for a more impressive-looking treat.

Hot chocolate gets a lively update with warming cinnamon and espresso.

cinnamon hot chocolate

PREP: 15 minutes   **SLOW COOK:** 4 hours (low)

6	**cups reduced-fat milk***
1½	**cups semisweet chocolate pieces**
1	**teaspoon instant espresso coffee powder**
1	**teaspoon ground cinnamon** **Ground cinnamon (optional)**

1. In a 3½- to 4-quart slow cooker combine milk, chocolate, coffee powder, and the 1 teaspoon cinnamon.

2. Cover and cook on low-heat setting for 4 hours, whisking vigorously once halfway through cooking time.

3. Whisk well before serving. If desired, sprinkle each serving with additional cinnamon. **Makes 12 servings.**

***Tip:** If you like, substitute your favorite nondairy milk alternative.

PER SERVING: 125 cal., 8 g fat (4 g sat. fat), 3 mg chol., 19 mg sodium, 16 g carb., 1 g fiber, 2 g pro.

index